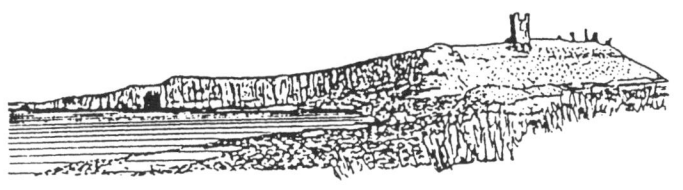

Northumbrian Coastline

Berwick-upon-Tweed to North Shields

Ian Smith

NORTHERN
HERITAGE

Acknowledgements.

My thanks go to all who have encouraged me to put pen to paper, and to all those who have loaned me photographs, shared their knowledge and offered accommodation.

To all of my family.

The section maps are to a scale of 1:45 000 and are based upon Landranger Map 75 (1984), Map 81 (1984) and Map 88 (1991) of the Ordnance Survey, with the permission of the Controller of Her Majesty's Stationery Office © Crown Copyright.

First published in Great Britain by Sandhill Press Ltd, 17 Castle Street, Warkworth, MORPETH, Northumberland, NE65 0UW, first edition in 1988, this edition in 1993.

© Ian Smith 1988, 1993.

First edition, first impression 1988
Second impression 1988
third impression 1989
fourth impression 1991
Second edition, first impression 1993
Second impression 1999
third impression 2010
fourth impression 2021

ISBN 978 0 955 54064 6

All rights reserved. No part of this publication may be reproduced, stored in a retrieval system, or transmitted in any form or by any means, electronic, mechanical, photocopying, recording or otherwise, without the prior permission of the copyright holder.

Printed and bound by Martins the Printers, Berwick upon Tweed

Contents

Preface to the Second Edition	4
Introduction	5
Rights of Way, Tides and Coastal Walking	9
Sensible Wear.	10
Accommodation.	11
Travel: Roads, Buses and Rail.	12
The Guide:	
— Marshall Meadows to Berwick.	14
• Berwick-upon-Tweed.	16
— Berwick to Holy Island Causeway.	22
• Lindisfarne (Holy Island).	30
— Holy Island Causeway to Bamburgh.	42
• Bamburgh.	50
— Bamburgh to Seahouses.	54
• Seahouses and the Farne Islands.	56
— Seahouses to Beadnell.	60
• Beadnell.	62
— Beadnell to Embleton.	64
• Embleton.	68
— Embleton to Dunstanburgh.	69
• Dunstanburgh Castle.	70
— Dunstanburgh to Howick.	73
• Howick Hall.	76
— Howick to Boulmer.	78
— Boulmer to Alnmouth.	81
— Alnmouth to Warkworth.	84
• Warkworth.	90
— Warkworth to Amble.	94
— Amble to Lynemouth : Druridge Bay.	96
— Lynemouth to Newbiggin.	104
• Newbiggin.	106
— Newbiggin to Blyth.	108
• Blyth Harbour.	114
— Blyth to Seaton Sluice.	116
• Seaton Sluice.	120
— Seaton Sluice to Whitley Bay.	122
• Cullercoats.	126
— Cullercoats to Tynemouth.	128
• Tynemouth Castle and Priory.	130
— Tynemouth to North Shields.	132
• North Shields.	134
Bibliography.	139
Index.	140
Symbols used on sketch maps	142.

Preface to the Second Edition

Five years on from the first edition, the Northumberland coastline is still magnificent, still beautiful. It has changed in small ways of course: the pressures of changing industry and commerce have altered its ports; growing awareness of conservation and wildlife issues have increased visitor numbers (and, ironically, car parks). But in the large frame this landscape is just the same: sweeping beaches; historic castles; the ever-changing sea and sky. It is still largely secret, waiting for you to get away from your transport and discover it.

This revised edition includes a few of the more obvious changes, and probes into some of the places that were met only briefly in the first edition. The "missing" pieces of the Northumberland coast have been added too: the border cliffs between Marshall Meadows and Berwick, and the peninsula beside Warkworth Harbour.

Many thanks to those who have written to mention their experiences along the coastline, and for the helpful comments.

Ian Smith

(June 1993).

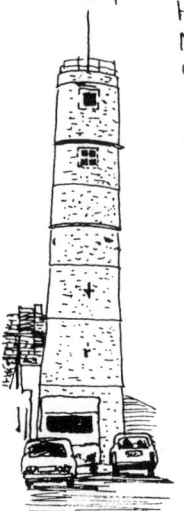

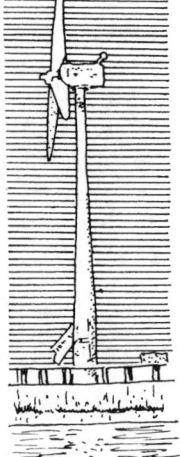

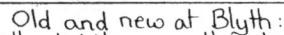

Old and new at Blyth:
- the lighthouse in the street (1788);
- the Port Authority's wind generators (1993)

INTRODUCTION

Northumberland keeps its coast secret from the casual passer-by. From the A1 there are tantalising glimpses of the sea and the Farne Islands. From the train there are sudden views of Alnmouth: red roofs and white sands. There are dramatic panoramas across Fenham Flats to Holy Island, and clifftop scenes near Berwick. Even from the coastal roads the shore itself stays hidden behind the dunes once you are north of the Wansbeck.

But if you are not in a hurry, if you are prepared to leave your car or bus or train and walk a little, there is much to discover. This guide is intended to encourage you to explore.

Beyond those dunes stretch vast beaches of glorious sand: Druridge Bay is seven miles of golden strand; Blyth, Warkworth, Alnmouth and Embleton have long golden sands too, whilst Bamburgh Beach has miles of silky white sand.

On Cresswell Beach

There is enough beach for everyone here. Even on hot days, with several hundred people along Druridge Bay you may be a quarter-mile or so from the next person. Yet even in winter they are seldom totally deserted.

Between the beaches are short sections of cliff, where the harder rocks resist the erosion of the elements. Here the bones of the land lie revealed. Geologists, and indeed anyone with any appreciation of rocks or patterns will enjoy these stretches. The various layers of rock lie open to inspection, forming wicked reefs across or along the shore, or great pavements revealed by the retreating tide. There are swirls of colour and texture in the cliffs as one rock succeeds another.

Small but fascinating bays huddle between headlands of resistant rock, and rock-pools offer a fascinating habitat to observe.

Rock strata and pools, by Rumbling Kern Howick

Hard rock is the base for the coast's best-known landmarks too: the great castles of Bamburgh, Dunstanburgh and Lindisfarne sit on outcrops of the Whin Sill. These remind us of the county's border status (as do the castles at Berwick, Warkworth and Tynemouth, plus the many inland castles).

Warkworth Castle

But the history of this region is expressed not just by reminders of war. The Celtic tradition of Christianity, nurtured on Holy Island, expanded from here, leaving much more than a few buildings and a local name for eider ducks!

Industry too has made its mark. It is still very obvious in the South-Eastern corner of the County, where there is still a continuing cycle of new industry replacing old. Lynemouth is very obviously industrial, with its coal-processing plant, power station and aluminium smelter. Seaton Sluice, on the other hand, seems remote from industrial influence. Yet this was the very heart of Northumberland's industry for centuries, until quite recently. Even Holy Island had its limestone, with quarries, tramways, kilns and export quay, at one time. Fascinating reminders of this industrial heritage lie scattered along the coast for the observant to find.

Fishing is one industry that has declined markedly. Boats still ply from the many little harbours and havens, but relatively few now. The great herring fleets have disappeared, leaving the distinctive deep-prowed cobles for the local specialised catches, and a handful of trawlers operating from the larger ports.

Tractor and trailer wait to land a coble, at Newbiggin

The coastal villages have their own character too. Most are exposed to the blasts from the North Sea. They sit firmly anchored on outcrops of rock, with inter-tidal rocks breaking the fury of the sea. But they have a rugged, austere look. Some, such as Bamburgh and Warkworth, are sheltered from the sea and have a softer, more rural appearance.

Near the Tyne the villages have run together to form a continuous but variegated townscape: Cullercoats is still distinct from its neighbours — Whitley Bay and Tynemouth.

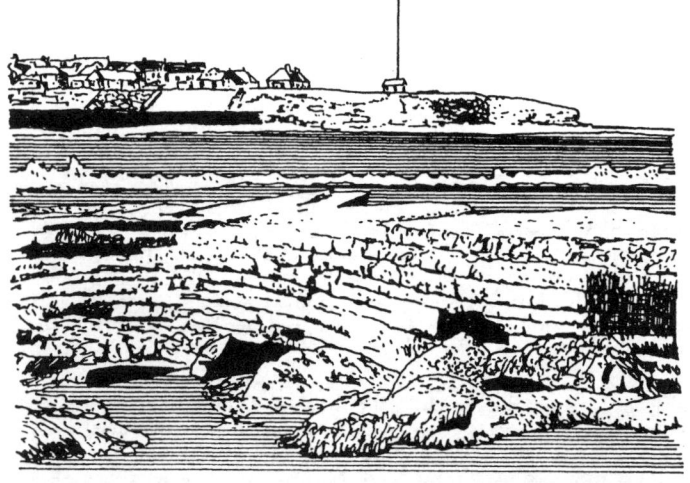

Cullercoats

The Guide

This includes a continuous strip map of the coast to a scale of 1:45 000, from the Border to North Shields, with notes and comments to assist those who want to walk along this coast and discover its secrets and joys.

It is not intended as a single long-distance walk. Much more of the coastal character can be appreciated by a series of short walks, taking time to stop, look and explore. Picking your way along the rock pools is more rewarding than eating up the miles. The buses serving the coast allow a wide range of one-way walks if carefully planned.

RIGHTS OF WAY, TIDES and COASTAL WALKING

The route indicated on the sketch maps is NOT evidence of a right of way. The shore between the tide-lines is mainly the property of the Crown, and there is seldom any objection to its use as a thoroughfare on foot. BUT it is not always passable or safe. There are many sections of the coastal walk where the best route is along the beach, so choose the time of your trips carefully to match the tide. (Tide times are published in the local newspapers). Avoid being trapped against cliffs or private property by the incoming tide. In particular take care on the flats of Goswick, Fenham and Budle Bay: the tide rushes in very quickly over the flat sands.

Major river crossings are made by bridge or ferry. But several of the smaller streams that flow into the sea can offer awkward or dangerous crossings. Be prepared to make a diversion if the conditions are against a safe passage.

Berwick Old Bridge

Notes on route-finding are brief. Except on the diversions inland the sea itself is a fairly reliable guide to the coastline and there is little scope for mistakes.

Rights of way ARE indicated on Ordnance Survey Maps. Useful sheets are:

1:50 000 Sheet 75, Berwick upon Tweed
Sheet 81, Alnwick and Morpeth
Sheet 88, Tyneside.

These sheets also offer much other information about the areas inland from the coast, and about the relief of the coastal strip itself, and can add much to your understanding and appreciation of what you see.

When using field paths or lanes, respect the countryside:
- Shut gates.
- Keep dogs under control. Where there is livestock keep them on a lead.
- Stay on the path. Do not wander on the crops. Remember that grass is an expensive and important crop!
- Guard against fire.
- Leave farm machinery, boats, crops and livestock alone.
- Take your litter home. Even a can ring-pull or a plastic bag can maim or kill.
- Respect wildlife, animals, sea-creatures, plants and trees. There is much to see, especially bird-life and flowers. Look, but do not interfere.

Below the bathing house, Howick

SENSIBLE WEAR

The weather along the coast can change very rapidly. A snow squall can reach you from the horizon quicker than you can walk a mile back to shelter. A hot summer's day can become distinctly chilly if the wind gets up from the sea. The descent of the North Sea roak, as cool sea air creeps in under still, warm land air to produce a belt of fog, brings both cold and loss of visibility to too many summer days.

So be prepared. In summer pack your cagoule and pullover as well as your sun-tan cream and swim-wear!
In winter, when the sea breeze can be bitterly cold, thermal wear, anoraks, woollen hats and mittens can be essential.

Sensible foot-wear needs thought too. Heavy boots are not the best wear for soft sandy beaches. Mud-flats may require wellingtons. Rocks and clifftops require more than town shoes or sandals. Select your footwear to match the route ahead.

Also remember to carry a watch: tides and buses wait for no man!
Binoculars are very useful too: there are large numbers of birds to see, and passing shipping.

ACCOMMODATION

There are villages every few miles along the coast, with inns, hotels and bed-and-breakfast accommodation. In summer this can be heavily booked, so it is wise to book ahead. The information centres may be able to help with addresses and telephone numbers.

Cottages and caravans can be hired at some locations. Campsites at Beachcomber, Waren Mill and Beadnell are conveniently situated. The Wansbeck Riverside Park at Ashington is inland but pleasant.

Caravanners fare somewhat better. In addition to the Ashington park there are sites at East Ord (near Berwick), Haggerston Castle, Waren Mill, Seahouses, Beadnell, Sandy Bay (Newbiggin) and near Whitley Bay.

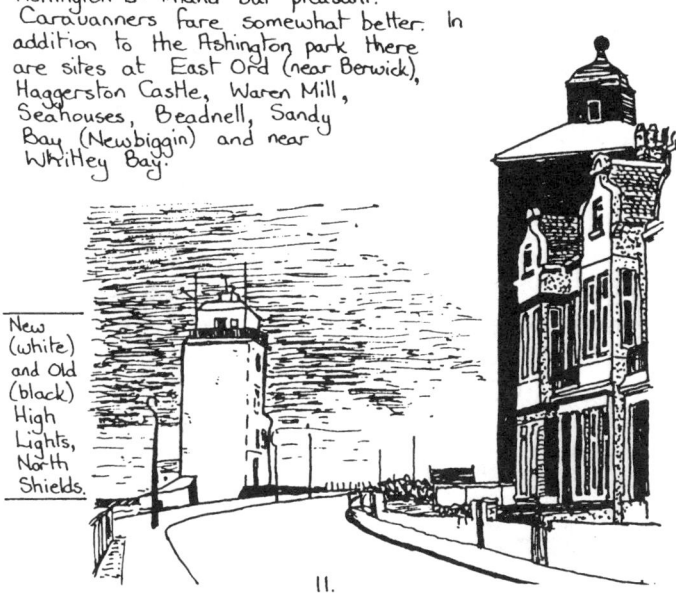

New (white) and Old (black) High Lights, North Shields.

Roads and Buses.

The coast is seldom far from a road, and a network of buses parallels it closely.

The Newcastle to Berwick service is very useful, linking many parts of the coast either directly or via changes at Belford, Alnwick or Morpeth.

There are buses to Holy Island some days.

A good service links Belford with Alnwick via Bamburgh, Seahouses, Beadnell, and Craster.

Other services link Alnwick through Alnmouth, Warkworth, Amble and Widdrington, to Morpeth or Ashington.

Cresswell, Lynemouth and Newbiggin have services to Ashington and/or Newcastle.

There is a sparse service to Cambois and North Blyth.

From Blyth southwards there is a frequent service of buses on the coast road through Seaton Sluice, Whitley Bay and Tynemouth.

Bus routes and times are subject to frequent change.

12.

Rail Travel

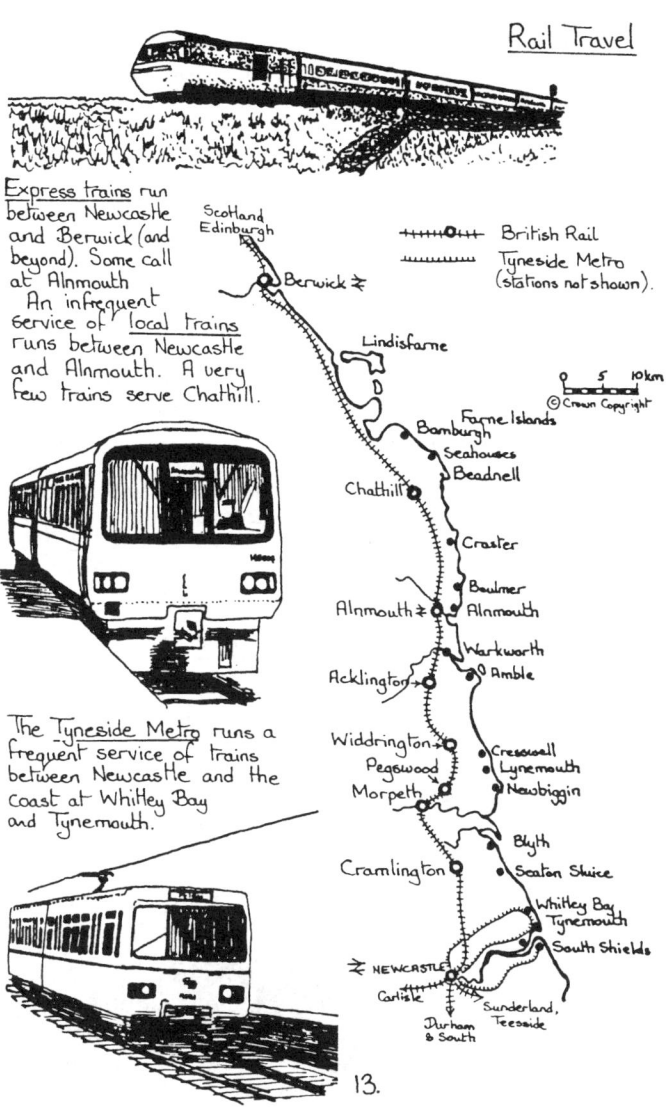

Express trains run between Newcastle and Berwick (and beyond). Some call at Alnmouth.

An infrequent service of local trains runs between Newcastle and Alnmouth. A very few trains serve Chathill.

The Tyneside Metro runs a frequent service of trains between Newcastle and the coast at Whitley Bay and Tynemouth.

++++O+++ British Rail
‿‿‿‿‿ Tyneside Metro (stations not shown).

13.

Marshall Meadows to Berwick.   9.3km, (5¾ miles).

* Marshall Meadows is easy to reach by bus from Berwick — or you may care to start a little further afield, from Burnmouth just over the Border.

Purists will make their way to the actual border, identified by the signs on the railway, before heading south along the coastal path.

At Marshall Meadows skirt the edge of the caravan and camp site in company with the railway, then escape to the cliff-edge. The path undulates south-eastwards along the edge. The Needle's Eye, a notable sea-bird roost, is passed. Berwick, visible ahead, gets closer, but very slowly!

Murphy's Beach is a change: golden sand below the cliffs. Beyond, Sharper's Head is crammed with caravans. But the next bay is delightful, with a small harbour and sandy beach. Choose whether to stay aloft, on the edge of the golf links, or descend to the beach round to the next headland. There, from the Redoubt, you can look across the flat fields of fire to the massive defences of Berwick. A ditch and bank — the "Covered Way", link the Redoubt to Brass Bastion and the Cow Port. You could enter the town that way, but you can also continue along the cliffs, descending to visit the pier (if safe) before entering Berwick through the Ness Gate.

The Needle's Eye.

Marshall Meadows to Berwick

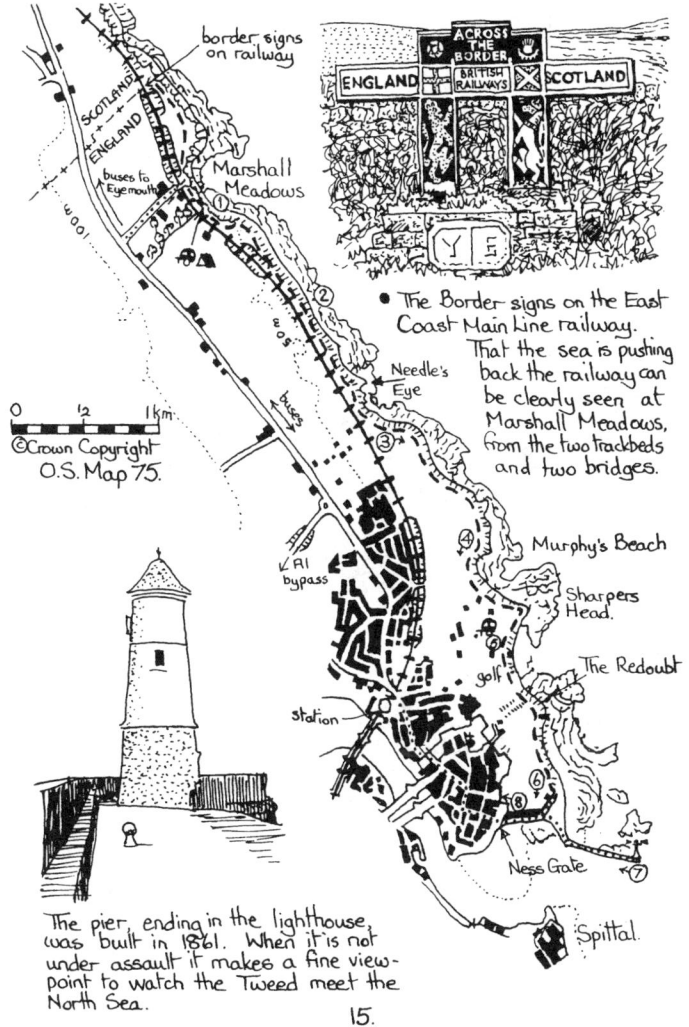

The Border signs on the East Coast Main Line railway. That the sea is pushing back the railway can be clearly seen at Marshall Meadows, from the two trackbeds and two bridges.

The pier, ending in the lighthouse, was built in 1861. When it is not under assault it makes a fine viewpoint to watch the Tweed meet the North Sea.

15.

<u>Berwick upon Tweed</u> is a very Scottish town, for all that it is now in England. It is an English town but a Scottish royal burgh. It is in Northumberland, but just to the north is the Scottish District of Berwickshire. Its football team plays in the Scottish League, its banks are mainly Scottish, yet its police, schools and local buses are English (or, rather, Northumbrian!). Geographically it ought to be in Scotland, for it lies on the north bank of the Tweed. It is armies and politics that have diverted the border a few miles to the north. In the past it has changed hands between the kingdoms (until 1482 thirteen times) and has from time to time been accorded a status alongside the larger divisions of the U.K. Thus Berwick declared war on Russia in the Crimean War, but was left out of the peace treaty! (This situation was formally remedied only in 1992!).

As a border town it has its own unique flavour. Enjoy a circuit of the Elizabethan ramparts before heading south.

The Royal Border Bridge
(before the electrification masts).

● Berwick Castle dates back to Edward I. It occupies a mound at the top of the town, overlooking both town and river. It was supplanted by the Elizabethan fortifications, but suffered most when the railway was built through it! A long curtain wall stretches down to a gun-position by the river.

> ✷ From the west side of the railway station bridge a path goes down through pleasant gardens past the Castle ruins. The path seems to be going to take you upriver, but below the hedge at the bottom a path runs back towards town. It passes through short tunnels under the ruined battery and becomes a pleasant walk under river-side trees, below the cliffs and walls that protect the town.

● The Royal Border Bridge, built in 1847, is 40m (126') high. There was much consternation at the prospect of electrification masts before 1990, with several amazing alternatives suggested (including freewheeling in from the south, and various towing devices!)

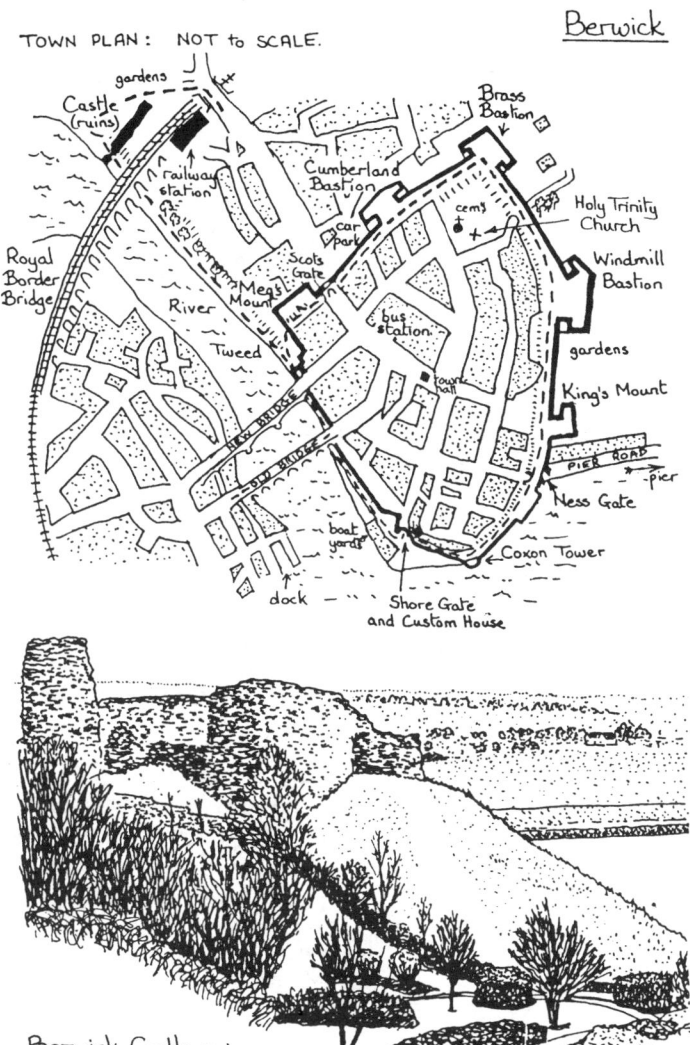

Berwick

* Continue along the riverside path towards the road bridges. On your left, above the trees, the natural walls and banks rise up to the fortifications of Megs Mount. On the river you will probably see swans in large numbers. Go on past the rowing-club house, and go under the first road-bridge.

- The New Bridge (or Royal Tweed Bridge officially) is a solid twentieth century essay in concrete. It was opened in 1928 to relieve the older bridge of the heavy traffic of the A1 (which nowadays crosses the river upstream at East Ord).
- More interesting is the Old Bridge — fifteen arches striding across the river. It dates back to 1611-24, and is reputed to have been built following caustic comments by James I (James VI of Scotland). He had to cross the river on the previous rickety wooden bridge on his way south to take up the throne of England. Certainly a new, solid bridge over the Tweed was a good symbol of the new United Kingdom.

* Cross the road at the north end of the Old Bridge, and follow the footpath along the housefronts atop Quay Walls. This gives a good view down over the quays and boatyards. (There is access to the riverside by steps beside the Shoregate Arch).

The New Bridge, from Meg's Mount.

Berwick.

* Keep on the walls beyond Shoregate, passing the Custom House to reach the Main Guard. Here a long line of gun platforms shows where the battery to command the river was sited...

Coxon's Tower (left) is next, followed by <u>Fisher's Fort</u> — both with fine views to the rivermouth. The Ness, on the north bank, ends with a pier and lighthouse, whilst the headland on the south shore is dominated by the factory chimney at Spittal.
  The path turns north, and climbs up over Ness Gate and up onto King's Mount.

● Russian cannon, Fisher's Fort. Captured at Sebastopol (Crimea) — its pair is on the promenade at Dartmouth (Devon). Note the wheels.

Berwick

- The Elizabethan ramparts are a symbol of the artillery age. Gone are the thin curtain walls of mediæval stone castles. They are replaced by thick earth-works, with a network of tunnels. A series of bastions protects the wall — and each other. Cannon hidden in the flankers can hail withering fire on anyone foolish enough to attack the walls. Careful geometry ensures that every wall is so protected. The ramparts are now in the care of English Heritage, who also maintain an infantry museum in the Barracks.

Berwick.

* Follow the ramparts round the northern side of the town. In succession you will pass King's Mount, Windmill, Brass & Cumberland Bastions. (At none of them is the named object visible!) The gardens, greens, views and trees make this a very attractive walk.

The wall brings you to Scot's Gate, where you cross over above the old Great North Road to Meg's Mount (named after Queen Margaret). This is a superb vantage point for views over the bridges and the town.

You can descend into town by Scots Gate, if you wish to visit the shops or other places of interest (such as the Town Hall (left), or the towerless Parish Church - built in the Commonwealth period).

Otherwise, a footpath descends to the New Bridge. The Old Bridge offers a way south that carries less road traffic.

— Scots Gate; Meg's Mount.

Berwick to Spittal (Sandstell Point)   2.4km (1½ miles).

* You have a choice of bridges leaving Berwick: the older lower bridge is perhaps more aesthetically pleasing to the pedestrian — and more romantic — but the New Bridge does offer better views, upstream to the Royal Border Bridge, and down-stream over the old bridge towards the river-mouth.
If you do choose the higher bridge, bear left at its south end past a little garden, and down the slope to meet the road from the lower bridge.
Follow the road through Tweedmouth, past the dock with its attendant warehouses. Continuing, you can walk along a grassy promenade beside the river. This is where the railway sidings and incline up to the main line used to be. You can see the level of the latter by the track maintenance depot up the hill. An archway on the right shows where the line crossed a road on one leg of its zigzag descent. (The bridge over the lower road has been demolished.)
The river is home to very many swans. You may also see cormorants perching on the pilings, and other seabirds.
Go on past the lifeboat station and pick a way out past the factory to Sandstell Point, at the mouth of the Tweed.

Tweedmouth Lifeboat-house

Berwick to Spittal

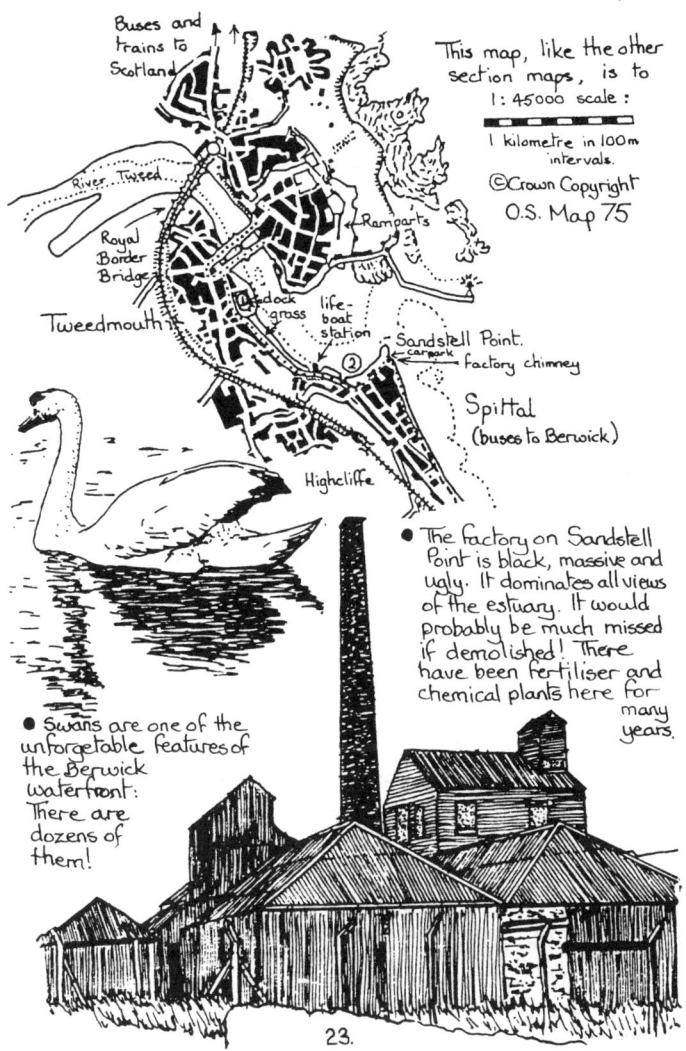

This map, like the other section maps, is to 1:45000 scale:

1 kilometre in 100m intervals.

©Crown Copyright O.S. Map 75

Buses and trains to Scotland

River Tweed

Royal Border Bridge

Tweedmouth

dock grass

lifeboat station

Ramparts

Sandstell Point
carpark
factory chimney

Spittal (buses to Berwick)

Highcliffe

- The factory on Sandstell Point is black, massive and ugly. It dominates all views of the estuary. It would probably be much missed if demolished! There have been fertiliser and chemical plants here for many years.

- Swans are one of the unforgetable features of the Berwick waterfront: There are dozens of them!

23.

Sandstell Point to Scremerston Seahouse. 3.3km (2 miles)

✳ The grassy path past the factory takes you to <u>Spittal Promenade</u>. A sandy beach is separated from a terrace of houses by a wall and a road. Walk on past the 'Pavilion' – a little entertainment centre – and the rest of the little resort. Near the end of promenade a path slants upwards (above and behind a block of toilets.) It joins a track that continues up onto the clifftops. You may see trains here: the electrified East Coast Main Line runs parallel to your path for a way.

The slope of the cliffs is determined by the dip-slope of the Scremerston Series of rocks. The wide variety of rocks is very obvious, and there are signs of mining in past times: ruins and pony <u>tracks</u>. Follow the track past Seahouse.

Cliffs towards Sea House

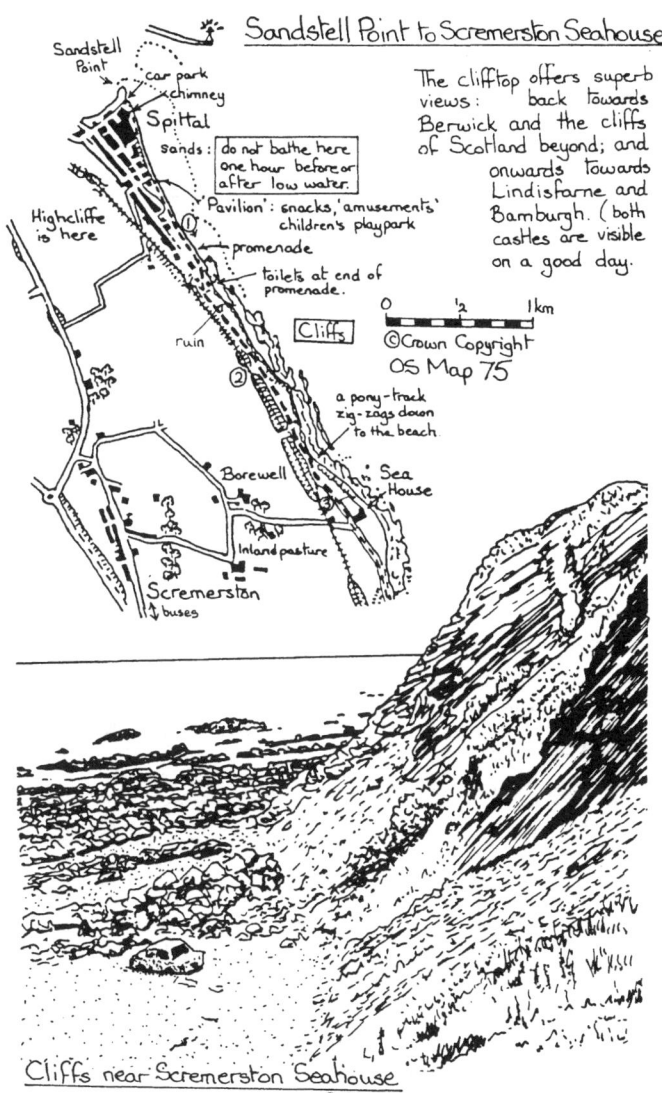

Sandstell Point to Scremerston Seahouse

The clifftop offers superb views: back towards Berwick and the cliffs of Scotland beyond; and onwards towards Lindisfarne and Bamburgh. (both castles are visible on a good day.)

Sandstell Point — car park — chimney — Spital — sands: do not bathe here one hour before or after low water. — Highcliffe is here — 'Pavilion': snacks, 'amusements' children's playpark — promenade — toilets at end of promenade — ruin — Cliffs — a pony-track zig-zags down to the beach — Borewell — Sea House — Inland pasture — Scremerston ↓ buses

© Crown Copyright OS Map 75

Cliffs near Scremerston Seahouse

25.

Scremerston Sea House to Cheswick Links 4.0km (2½ miles)

Cocklawburn Beach.

* Follow the lane down from Sea House to Cocklawburn Beach. Note how the rock strata are in a different direction ahead: instead of running parallel to the shoreline and forming the dip-slope of the cliffs, now they stick out from the shore as a series of fangs. If the tide permits, the shore is the best route as it takes you over one set of rock and then another. Here are different colours, shapes, textures. There are slabs of limestone pavement; hard, pale-grey and jointed into blocks. There are tilted beds of limestone lumps sitting on top of sandstone. There are jagged areas of different-coloured sandstones, — and golden sand between.

If the tide is high, you may have to follow the lane to its end, and the rough trackway over the dunes.

Beyond the prominent ruinous limekiln the beach starts to settle down to uniformity; golden sands backed by dunes. This scenery is much in evidence between here and Cresswell Ahead of you the castles of Lindisfarne and Bamburgh may be visible if the weather is kind.

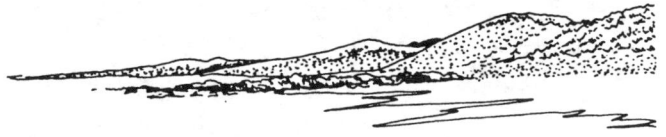

Cheswick Black Rocks, and the dunes.

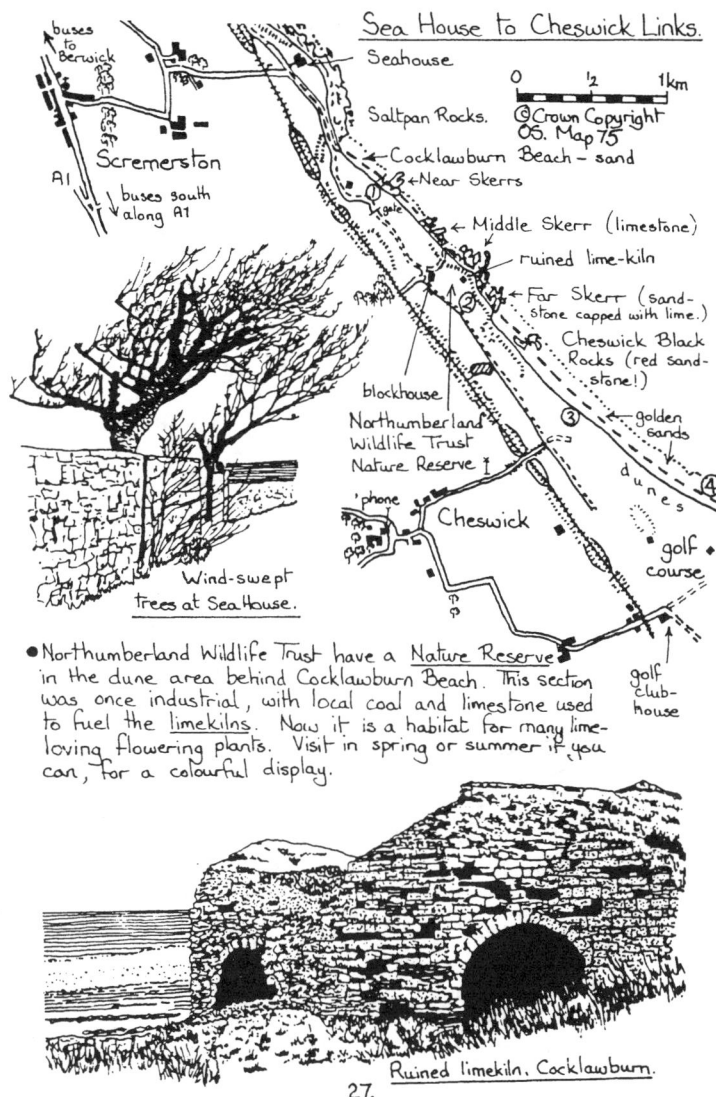

Sea House to Cheswick Links.

- Seahouse
- Saltpan Rocks
- Cocklawburn Beach – sand
- Near Skerrs
- Middle Skerr (limestone)
- ruined lime-kiln
- Far Skerr (sandstone capped with lime.)
- Cheswick Black Rocks (red sandstone!)
- golden sands
- dunes
- golf course
- blockhouse
- Northumberland Wildlife Trust Nature Reserve
- Cheswick
- golf club-house

© Crown Copyright OS. Map 75

Scremerston — buses to Berwick / buses south along A1

Wind-swept trees at SeaHouse.

- Northumberland Wildlife Trust have a <u>Nature Reserve</u> in the dune area behind Cocklawburn Beach. This section was once industrial, with local coal and limestone used to fuel the <u>limekilns</u>. Now it is a habitat for many lime-loving flowering plants. Visit in spring or summer if you can, for a colourful display.

Ruined limekiln, Cocklawburn.

Cheswick Links to Holy Island Causeway 6.3km, (4 miles)

Cheswick Beach and the dune islands

* Walking south-east along the beach it is easy to miss the point where the actual shore-line turns south to Cheswick Golf Club, and Goswick. This is because the long bar of sand that stretches out towards Holy Island is quite high. Except when the tide is high you may not see over it if you follow the water's edge.

Ahead are two solitary tall dunes, capped with grass. These become islands at the top of the tide, as evidenced by the debris strewn over the sands. A lagoon then separates them from the shore.

According to tide, weather and your own whims you can decide where to cross to follow the main shoreline. (North Low appears to sink into the sands of the lagoon). You may wish to follow the beach along past Beachcomber House (with the lookout tower) — or go along the road past Goswick. This continues as a track and then as a public field-path. But the dunes separate it from all views of the sea.

Beachcomber House

* Beyond the point you have an excellent view across the sands and/or water to Holy Island. Follow the shore path (or field path) south to meet and cross South Low — see the notes opposite!

A squelchy path will take you on round Beal Point towards the Holy Island Causeway. You approach the road by picking a route between huge concrete blocks, to reach the tide-tables.

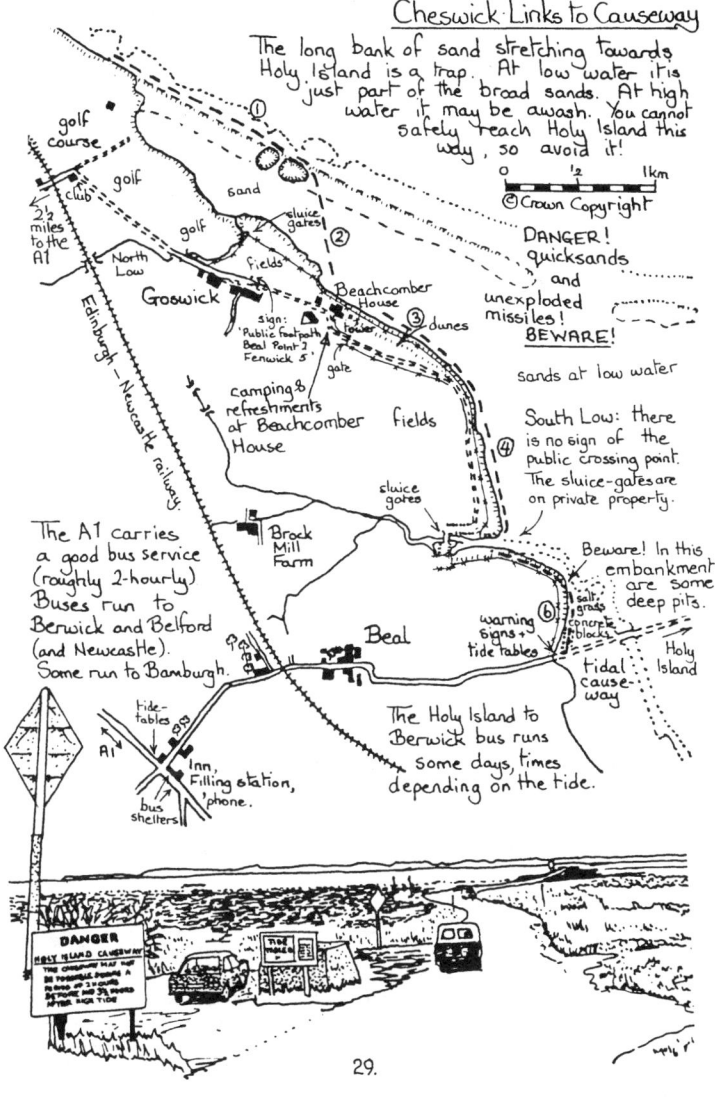

Lindisfarne: a circular detour. 17.7km (11 miles)

The digression onto Holy Island is a must. Here is one of the ancient centres of British culture. Here during the Dark Ages Christianity took root. This little island had a reputation for learning throughout Europe.
Even if history bores you there is much to see on Lindisfarne.

Another mile to the A1
Beal

But this trip does require careful planning. The island is cut off from the mainland for about half of each tide.
The causeway is the only safe way onto or off the island, and then only during the specified crossing times. These can be found by consulting the tables at each end of the causeway, or by telephoning the Tourist Information Office.

Do make sure that you work out how long is available, whether you intend to be on the island and off again during one low-water period, or whether you plan to wait until the water drops again. Missing the tide, unplanned, can mean a long wait — and you may not fancy a crossing in the dark!
Every now and then someone disregards the timetable and gets caught on the causeway: the tide rises very fast, and runs strongly enough to push cars off the roadway: that's why the refuge box is there!

✱ Follow the causeway across to the Island, and along to the village. There you will find some shops catering for the tourist trade, selling the newly-traditional delights of Lindisfarne Liqueur, Lindisfarne Mead, Lindisfarne Fudge....., even a mead factory. There is also a post office, and several public houses and hotels.

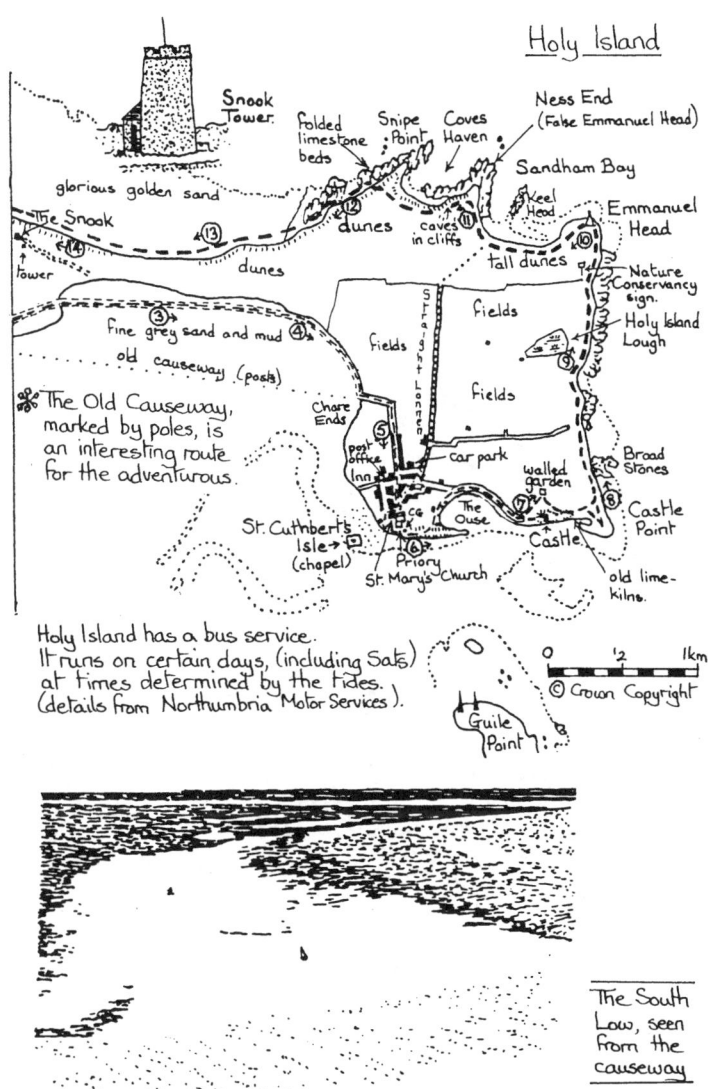

Holy Island

✿ The Old Causeway, marked by poles, is an interesting route for the adventurous.

Holy Island has a bus service. It runs on certain days, (including Sats) at times determined by the tides. (details from Northumbria Motor Services).

The South Low, seen from the causeway

Lindisfarne Priory

The 'rainbow'

Lindisfarne Priory

> * The Priory is at the south end of the village, beyond the square.

Saint Aidan arrived on Lindisfarne in 635 AD, at the behest of Oswald, king of Northumbria. He established a Priory in the Celtic tradition which flourished, being esteemed throughout Europe. St. Cuthbert was Prior here, and Bishop of Lindisfarne.

The Priory lasted until 875, when the Danes burned it. Nothing material remains except the chapel ruins on St Cuthbert's Island. But still the island affects its visitors, many of whom go away knowing just why it is called Holy Island.

- The ruins that you <u>do</u> see are of the later Priory. It was refounded by Benedictine monks from Durham Abbey in the 11th century. The architecture of the church is very similar to that of Durham Cathedral, with its carved alternating pillars. It was built at the same time. When complete it must have been a beautiful building, with Durham's form but rich red sandstone (from Cheswick). Even now it invokes awe.
- The monastic buildings are later again (13th century), and are in a grey sandstone. The Priory was appropriated by Henry <u>VIII</u>, who had it stripped of roof and valuables. Even its stone went to build the castle.
- To the west of the Priory is the <u>parish church of St Mary</u>. This was established in 1140. It is worth a visit, as is the <u>museum</u> by the entrance to the Priory.

33.

Lindisfarne

St. Mary's Church

> ✷ From St. Mary's Church go down the track towards the beach and St. Cuthbert's Island:

• <u>St. Cuthbert's Island</u> is semi-tidal. The ruins of the chapel there are the only remains of the Saxon Priory.
St. Cuthbert used to seclude himself on the islet (before resorting to the greater solitude of Inner Farne.) It is said that this holy man became well-loved by the local wildlife including seals, otters and the eider ducks that are still generally known in Northumberland as Cuddy's Ducks.

Lindisfarne

> ✴ Climb up onto the Heugh (the rocky ridge)

- The Heugh is a ridge of dolerite (like Whin Sill responsible for much of Northumberland's dramatic scenery.) On top is a Coastguard lookout. It has fine views over the Ouse towards the castle, and south over the Harbour to Guile Point, where the Beacons are prominent.

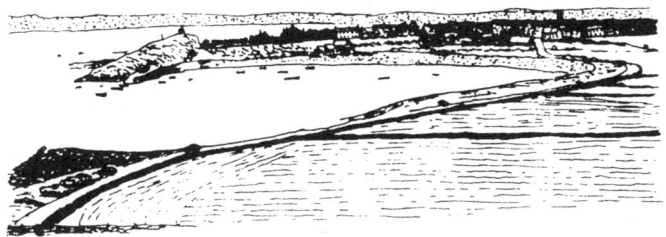

> ✴ From the Heugh follow a path down past the fishermen's sheds and pass their stores (made traditionally from upturned boats that have had their day). Follow round the shore of the Ouse to the road and go along to the Castle

- The stores on the east side of the Castle have their own history.. Before their inversion and division into three sections they formed the "Shetland Bus". This trawler plied back and forth across the North Sea to Norway during the Second World War, carrying news, agents and other passengers.

Lindisfarne Castle

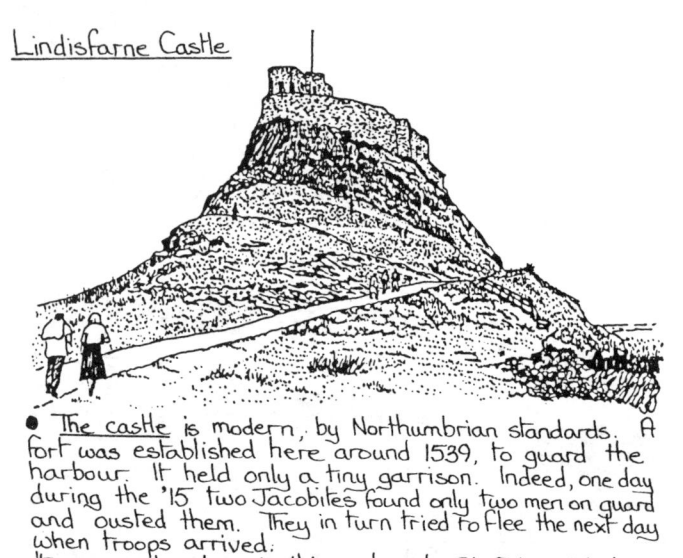

- <u>The castle</u> is modern, by Northumbrian standards. A fort was established here around 1539, to guard the harbour. It held only a tiny garrison. Indeed, one day during the '15 two Jacobites found only two men on guard and ousted them. They in turn tried to flee the next day when troops arrived.

  It was restored early this century by Sir Edward Lutyens, producing a romantic residence, perched atop a column of dolerite. Now it is in the care of the National Trust, who have the problem of its being over-worn by too many visitors!

- Just to the north is a <u>walled garden</u>, well worth a visit when open.

Lindisfarne's Lime Industry

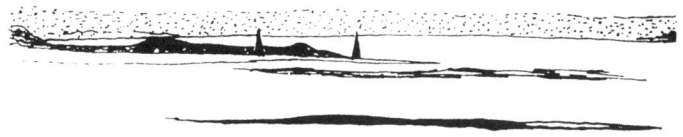

- The beacons on Guile Point, south across the Harbour, were built in the 1860s by a Dundee company to help its ships navigate past the shoals to the island's wharves. They brought in coal for the kilns and carried away the lime.

- The limekilns can be seen just east of the Castle. They are built back against another dolerite pillar. A tramway that brought limestone across from quarries on the north side of the island can be traced.

Holy Island: Castle to Causeway.

* Venture out onto Castle Point, to enjoy the views. Out to sea the Farne Islands are prominent with their lighthouses: red and white on Longstone; white on Inner Farne. Much more massive, Bamburgh Castle dominates the southern scene beyond the gold of Ross Back Sands.
* Follow the shore northwards to Emmanuel Head.

- Holy Island Lough, passed on your left, is fresh water. It has whooper swans in winter.

- That white triangle is not a yacht sail, but the day-mark on Emmanuel Head. It is 10m (30ft) high!

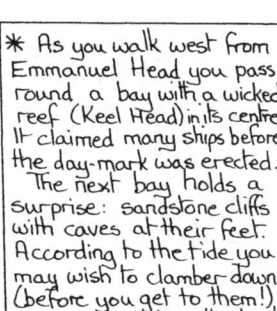

* As you walk west from Emmanuel Head you pass round a bay with a wicked reef (Keel Head) in its centre. It claimed many ships before the day-mark was erected.
The next bay holds a surprise: sandstone cliffs with caves at their feet. According to the tide you may wish to clamber down (before you get to them!), or saunter along the top.

Holy Island: Castle to Causeway

✽ Beyond Snipe Point you come to a bed of limestone, that gives some interesting arched formations. Then there is an immense beach of gold, that at low tide stretches to the horizon. But do not be tempted to head directly for Cheswick across the old ranges — there are quicksands as well as all kinds of unexploded horrors there.

Please do not clamber on the face of the dunes, as rapid erosion is caused. This area, beach and dunes, is part of the Lindisfarne Nature Reserve.

Go round the end of the island to the causeway. Check that you have enough time before starting to cross. Remember the refuge!

Lindisfarne Nature Reserve

- The Nature Conservancy Council manage the Nature Reserve comprising part of Holy Island and a vast inter-tidal area stretching down to Budle Bay. As this is below the high tide level, and there is no public footpath behind the beach in most places, visits must be carefully planned to avoid trespass.

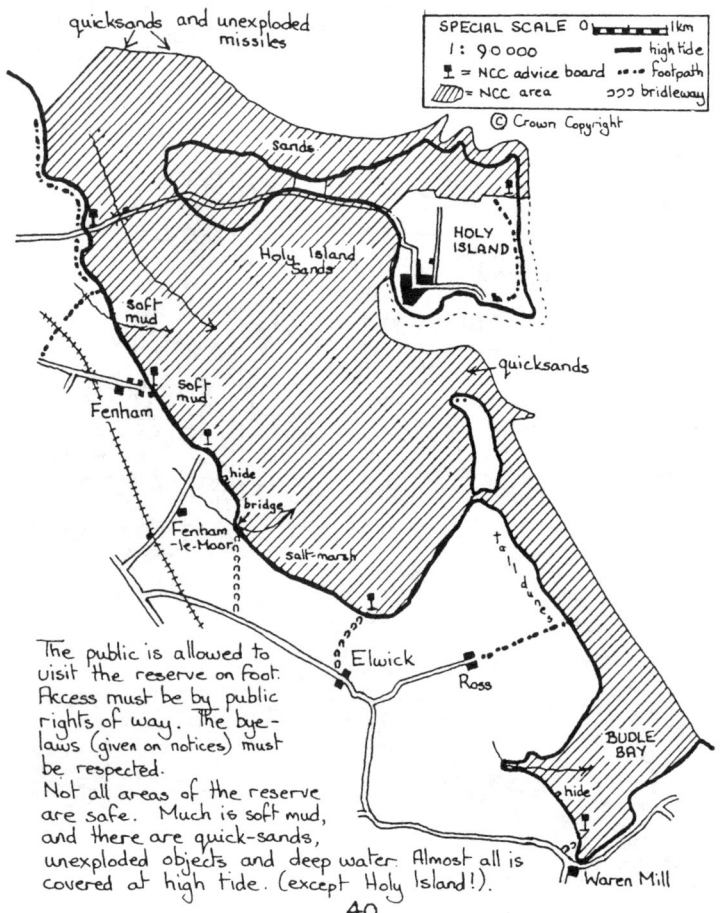

The public is allowed to visit the reserve on foot. Access must be by public rights of way. The bye-laws (given on notices) must be respected.

Not all areas of the reserve are safe. Much is soft mud, and there are quick-sands, unexploded objects and deep water. Almost all is covered at high tide. (except Holy Island!).

Lindisfarne Nature Reserve

Fenham (NOT in the Reserve!)

The reserve is best known for the variety of its wildfowl and wading birds. There are residents, winter visitors and passing migrants. Take a pair of binoculars and a bird book, and listen too — the lovely liquid call of the curlew is often to be heard over the Flats. Take your time, but remember the tide and your planned point of egress.

More information about the Reserve may be obtained from:
Regional Officer
Nature Conservancy Council
Archbold House
Archbold Terrace
NEWCASTLE upon TYNE
NE2 1EG

A hide overlooking Fenham Flats.

Holy Island Causeway to Elwick Shore. 12.4km (7¾ miles)

I expected this to be straightforward. Even though there is a distinct lack of public paths above the tide-line for most of the way the tidal zone offers open access. But Black Low proved impassable at the shore, and soft mud made progress past Fenham difficult to impossible. Diversions inland using rights-of-way had to be used.

✴ From the causeway head southwards, on a soggy path, from between the lines of concrete blocks. Look carefully for the start of the path up onto Fenham Hill - the stile may be missing. Cross the fields to the railway. Make sure that nothing is hurtling towards you at high speed, and cross the tracks. (The ballast is very wide as the curve has been flattened. The cant of the tracks is to allow very high speeds despite the curve.)
Follow the hedge up the hill to a lane, where you have a choice:
✻1: a simple route goes right briefly, then follows the lane past Fenwick Granary to the A1.
✴ If you prefer less of the main road follow the lane to Fenham. Beyond the farm (with its attractive trees) you pass a cluster of houses with well-kept gardens and a field of grassy mounds (There is a story under there somewhere). A narrow alley leads down to the shore.
✻2: Those who really like deep, soft, sticky mud may follow the shore.
✴ A field-path heads inland from just north of Fenham Farm. It goes past a prominent electricity pole to another crossing of the railway. (I hope you enjoy train-spotting). The burn beyond is more of a problem in wet weather. Go on up the slope, by the hedge, towards Fenwick Stead. At a belt of derelict trees head to the left of the farm-buildings. A lane takes you towards the A1, but you can go straight on at a corner, to the right of a hedge, up to a hidden stile onto the A1.
Fortunately there is a wide verge, with a rudimentary path in the grass, for the short walk past Buckton to the next seaward lane. Enjoy the extensive views, right over Holy Island. Even the beacon on Emmanuel Head may be seen. Go downhill again, over Lowmoor Crossing. Watch for birds in the hedgerows - this is a popular roost for migrants.
Beyond Fenham-le-Moor you reach a beach. Real sand! Follow it south round Tealhole Point. On the way you will pass a hide - on stilts as it is below the high water mark. A footbridge takes you over Fenham Burn. Turn down the steps to the shore <u>below</u> the embankment.
Follow the edge of the salt-marsh southwards, below the level of the raised fields, towards Elwick Shore.

Holy Island Causeway to Elwick Shore.

Map annotations:

- warning signs, tide tables and info →
- tidal causeway
- Holy Island
- refuge box
- concrete blocks
- hedge
- to Beal and the A1
- watch for this path
- South Low
- ①
- very soft mud
- Black Low
- Granary Point
- Fenham Hill ②
- hedge
- ③ ④
- Fenham
- NCC sign
- slipway (private)
- pylon
- very soft mud
- Fenwick Granary
- 5→10m high loose shale cliffs
- Lowmoor Point
- NCC sign
- hedge ⑤
- Fenham Burn
- ⑨ sand. hide. hut.
- Fenwick Stead
- Fenham-le-Moor
- Tealhole Point ⑩
- 0   ½   1km
- © Crown Copyright
- OS Map 75
- The A1 carries a good bus service between Berwick, Alnwick and Newcastle, with connections at Belford for Waren Mill, Bamburgh and the coast.
- ⑥ hedge
- stile
- ⑧ footbridge
- Lowmoor Crossing
- salt-marsh
- Buckton ⑦
- ⑪ rubble ⑫ NCC sign
- fields
- derelict windpump
- no bus
- Elwick

• At Buckton, in 1685, a Scots girl, Grizel Cochrane, held up the London Mail at pistol point. (She had taken the precaution of stealing the postman's pistols!) She seized the death-warrant against her father, jailed for insurrection.

43.

Elwick Shore to Ross Back Sands 7.1km (4½ miles)

The Beacons on Guile Point.

* From Elwick Shore the coast curves gently round to Guile Point. Behind the embankment are the low fields of Ross Farm, jealously guarded against the high tide. The farm is protected on the seaward side by 20 metre high dunes, while conifers combat the wind. Underfoot Spartina grass gives way to sand. At the gap before Old Law you should consider time and tide. The sea runs through here as high tide approaches, making Old Law an island. If you have timed it right continue along the soft sandy shore to the Beacons.

- Enjoy the views over the flats: to the Kyloe and Cheviot hills. Watch out for wildfowl — and wildfowlers too in their season! Lindisfarne comes back into view as you round Guile Point, with the Heugh and Castle prominent. But do not head out over the sands at low tide: there are quicksands.

* Follow the sea-shore southwards. Here is typical Northumberland coastal scenery: tall dunes and broad sands. Recross the gap at Ross Point and continue along the shore. Ahead now is Bamburgh Castle, a mirror image of Lindisfarne.

Elwick Shore to Ross Back Sands

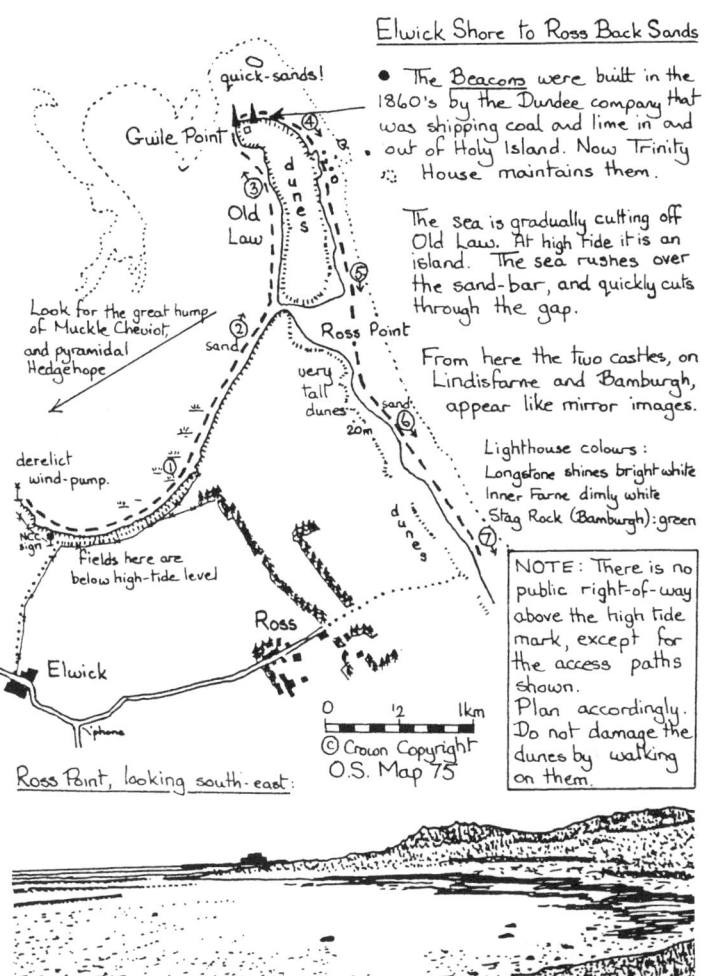

- The Beacons were built in the 1860's by the Dundee company that was shipping coal and lime in and out of Holy Island. Now Trinity House maintains them.

The sea is gradually cutting off Old Law. At high tide it is an island. The sea rushes over the sand-bar, and quickly cuts through the gap.

From here the two castles, on Lindisfarne and Bamburgh, appear like mirror images.

Lighthouse colours:
Longstone shines bright white
Inner Farne dimly white
Stag Rock (Bamburgh): green

NOTE: There is no public right-of-way above the high tide mark, except for the access paths shown.
Plan accordingly.
Do not damage the dunes by walking on them.

© Crown Copyright O.S. Map 75

Ross Point, looking south-east:

45.

Ross Back Sands to Waren Mill 4.3km (2¾ miles)

Wreck of a cement-laden barge on the sand-spit, Budle Bay

Budle Bay poses problems:
① The mouth of the bay, although narrow at low tide, is deep and dangerous. Lives have been lost here. Do NOT attempt to cross.
② Ross Low can be waded, with care, when the tide is out (and not after rain). But you need a taste for mud — of the ankle-deep, boot-sucking variety. Wellies are called for!
③ There is no right of way above the high tide mark. If the tide is in, or the river swollen, you cannot pass without trespass. So use the other, inland route, on the public footpath across Ross Links, and the lanes via Ross and Eastington.

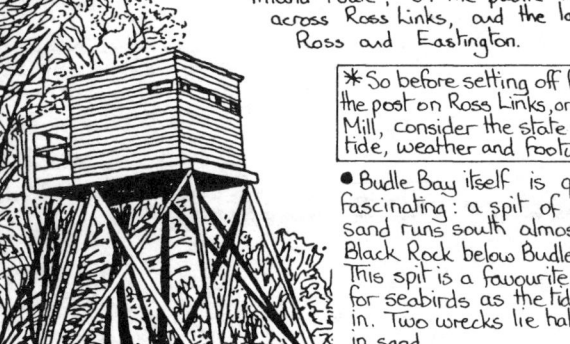

✻ So before setting off from the post on Ross Links, or Waren Mill, consider the state of the tide, weather and footwear.

• Budle Bay itself is quite fascinating: a spit of firm sand runs south almost to Black Rock below Budle Point. This spit is a favourite roost for seabirds as the tide comes in. Two wrecks lie half-buried in sand.
Inland, the summits of Cheviot and Hedgehope peep over the Kyloe Hills.

Ross Back Sands to Waren Mill

READ THE NOTES!

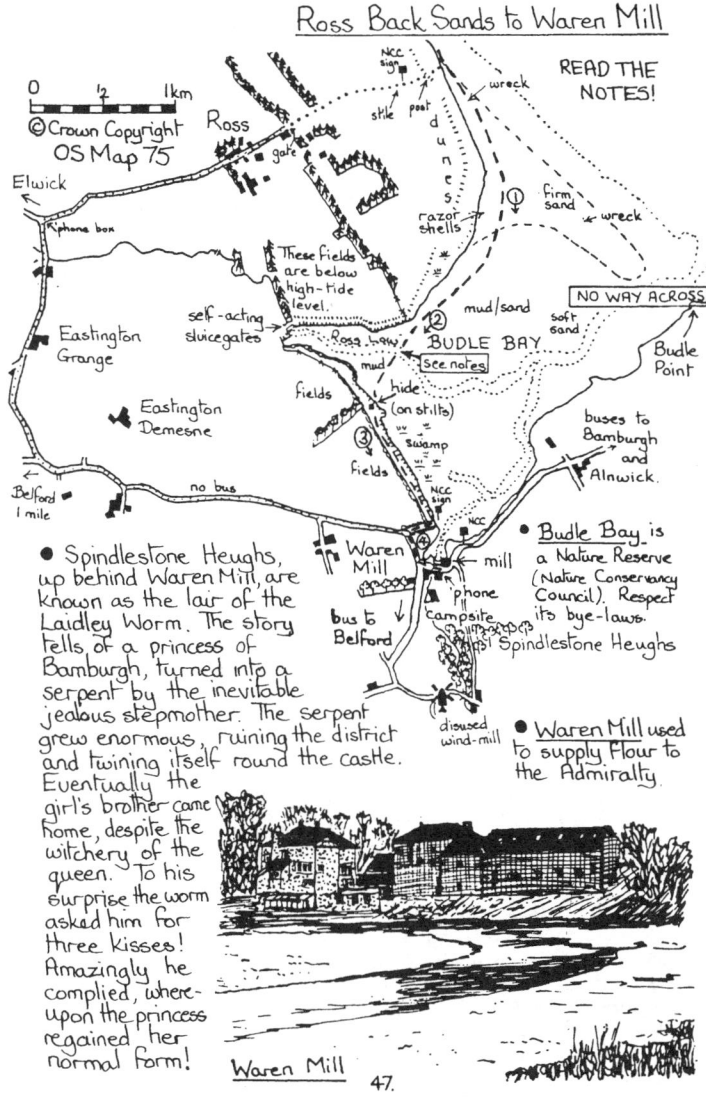

- Spindlestone Heughs, up behind Waren Mill, are known as the lair of the Laidley Worm. The story tells of a princess of Bamburgh, turned into a serpent by the inevitable jealous stepmother. The serpent grew enormous, ruining the district and twining itself round the castle. Eventually the girl's brother came home, despite the witchery of the queen. To his surprise the worm asked him for three kisses! Amazingly he complied, whereupon the princess regained her normal form!

- **Budle Bay** is a Nature Reserve (Nature Conservancy Council). Respect its bye-laws.

- **Waren Mill** used to supply flour to the Admiralty.

Waren Mill

47.

Waren Mill to Bamburgh. 5.7km (3½ miles)

Budle Point

Waren Mill still has the mill-buildings, and a large sheltered camp-site (with a shop and other amenities). There are buses to Belford and Berwick, and the other way to Bamburgh.

* From the mill follow the road alongside Budle Bay. A pair of binoculars and a bird-book are distinct assets here, as the bay supports huge numbers of birds as residents or visitors. Greylag geese and waders invade Chesterhill Slakes in winter, and large numbers of birds gather on the sands opposite.

At Budle, turn north down the track to the sea past some cottages. Enter the National Nature Reserve (note the sign), and turn east along the shore. The beach soon turns from stones to very fine sand. Pass Heather Cottages and the old quay (once a loading point for whinstone quarried from Kittling Hill). Continue along the beach to Black Rock, a large flat slab of dolerite that marks the end of Budle Bay.

The view north and west from Black Point is extensive, with Ross Links and Holy Island to the north, and the Kyloe Hills forming a backdrop to the glistening expanse of Budle Bay.

More sand, and mixed outcrops of rock below low cliffs are met on the way to Stag Point. A path leads up past the automatic lighthouse. Beyond, the rocky shoreline can be followed over Harkess Rocks, and on to the sandy beach, or the road can be followed into Bamburgh Village. The castle on its dolerite mound dominates the view (unless it is foggy!).

If the sea is angry or the tide very high, you may wish to use another route, from Heather Cottages, over Kittling Hill to the golf club-house, and then the road.

Bamburgh

- <u>Bamburgh</u> is not just a castle, although the massive edifice does dominate the village. The latter caters for holiday-makers, with accommodation, pubs, a coffee-house, shops, a post-office. In the centre is a triangular patch of greenery: a clump of trees. This is not a bad place to wait for a bus!

Buses run west to Belford and then Berwick (by connection or direct). They also go south to Seahouses, Embleton, Craster, Alnwick and Newcastle.

- <u>Saint Aidan's church</u> is a lovely place. It dates from the 13th century, replacing the previous building established for Aidan. It is a large church for a tiny village. Sit inside and ponder on the faith that produced it. The stained glass commemorates the saints of Northumbria. Outside is a Victorian memorial to Grace Darling.

Grace Darling   Bamburgh

was the daughter of the lighthouse keeper on Longstone, one of the Farne Islands. In the early light of 7th September 1838, when she was 23 years old, Grace was on watch during a gale. She saw a vessel - the Forfarshire - strike Big Harcar, and alerted her father. A little later, 7am, they spotted survivors on the rock. They decided that although they could not hope to row both ways in the wind, survivors might be able to help them to row back. They launched their coble, and found eight men and a woman on the rock - out of 52 on the vessel. They could not carry all of them, so took five initially. Two of the survivors helped them to make a second trip, so saving all nine.

The event made the Darlings national heroes, and Grace refused several offers of marriage to stay at the light. She died of consumption only four years later, despite kindness and hospitality from the Duchess of Northumberland.

- A large ornate memorial stands near the church door at Saint Aidan's, within sight of the sea. There is also a museum in Bamburgh of Grace Darling memorabilia, with the famous coble. More importantly, the public outcry resulted in better inspections for ships: all sailors have cause to thank Grace.

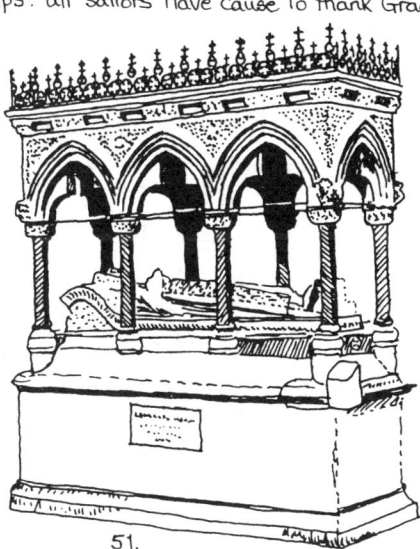

Grace Darling Memorial.
(minus railings).

Bamburgh Castle

* Access to Bamburgh Castle is gained from the drive that winds up under the southern walls to a gateway high on the eastern battlements

Bamburgh Castle is private property, but is opened to the public on summer afternoons. As well as the ramparts the apartments, kitchens and the museum of Lord Armstrong's work may be visited.

• The <u>gatehouse</u> (above) was Norman in origin, but like much of the castle has been restored from a ruinous condition.

• There has been a <u>castle</u> here since AD 547, when Ida, king of Northumbria, raised a wooden fortress on top of the 40 metre (130 feet) high block of Whin Sill. The site was really too good a defensive position to miss.
Ida's grandson, King Ethelfrith, gave it to his wife Bebba, giving rise to the name: Bebbanburgh.
The battlements give as good a view now as then of the Farne Islands.

Bamburgh Castle

- The massive keep was built by Henry I after Viking raids had destroyed the old wooden fort. Bamburgh stayed in royal hands and had an active history in the border wars. Here kings of England and Scotland met. Here queens were beseiged and held court.

Queen Margaret, wife of Henry VI, used this as her castle during the Wars of the Roses, until she rode away to fight — and lose — the Battle of Hexham.

Eventually James I gave it away, to the Forsters of Addlestone, Wardens of the Eastern March, who held it for a hundred years. Lord Crewe, Bishop of Durham, who married Dorothy Forster, bought it in 1704 and began the task of restoring the ruins. Lord Armstrong, the Tyneside inventor eventually bought it and "improved" it to its present condition.

The Castle's view north-west over Stag Rock and to Scotland.

Bamburgh to Seahouses   6.1km, (3¾ miles)

Bamburgh Castle, from the beach

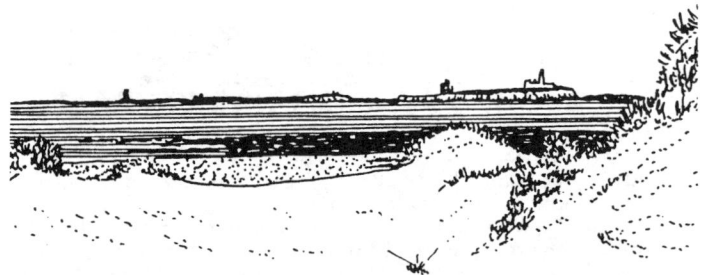

A gap in the dunes reveals the Farne Islands, beyond the Islestone.

Monks House

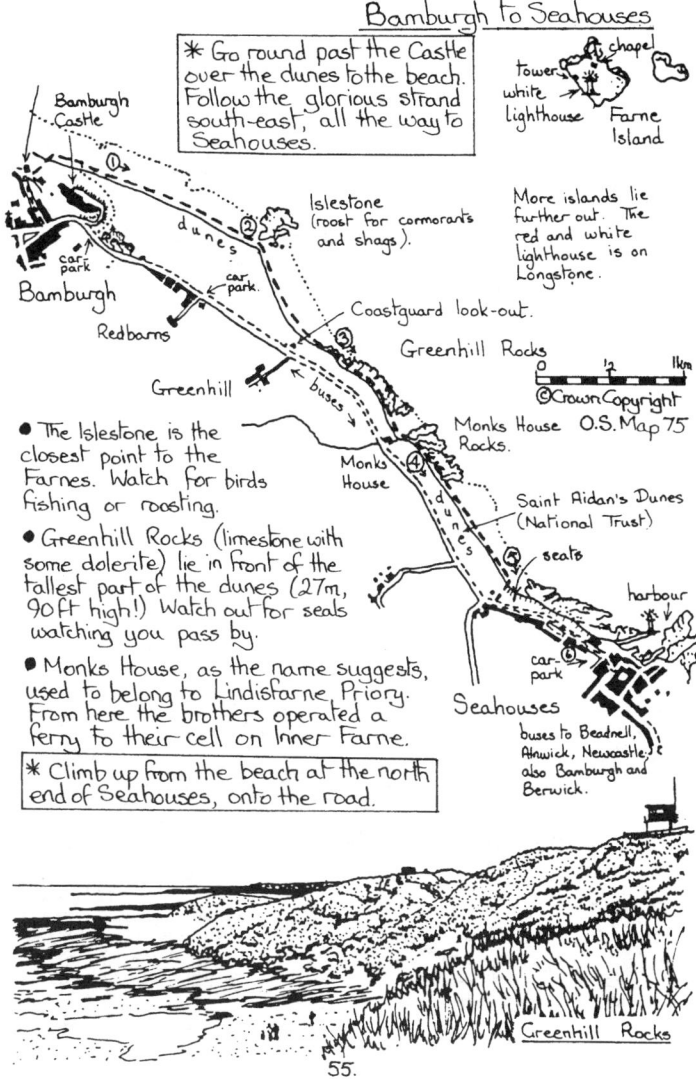

Bamburgh to Seahouses

* Go round past the Castle over the dunes to the beach. Follow the glorious strand south-east, all the way to Seahouses.

More islands lie further out. The red and white lighthouse is on Longstone.

- The Islestone is the closest point to the Farnes. Watch for birds fishing or roosting.

- Greenhill Rocks (limestone with some dolerite) lie in front of the tallest part of the dunes (27m, 90ft high!) Watch out for seals watching you pass by.

- Monks House, as the name suggests, used to belong to Lindisfarne Priory. From here the brothers operated a ferry to their cell on Inner Farne.

* Climb up from the beach at the north end of Seahouses, onto the road.

Seahouses buses to Beadnell, Alnwick, Newcastle, also Bamburgh and Berwick.

Greenhill Rocks

Seahouses

- The harbour at Seahouses uses a natural haven in a band of hard rocks (as can be seen at low tide), reinforced by modern harbour walls. The extensive flat rocks also protect the otherwise exposed town from the fury of the North Sea.
Here in summer you will find fish and chips, candy floss, oversized lollipops and "kiss-me-quick" hats. Meals and accommodation are available, as are car parking, shops and Information.
- Not to be missed: (a) the harbour; (b) a trip to the Farnes.

Seahouses Harbour

The Farne Islands

- If the weather is clear you cannot fail to notice them, as you walk the coast. They are the easternmost outcrop of the Whin Sill, the hard basalt resisting erosion by the sea to leave a scattered group of islands over an area 4km by 3km.

The islands are home — or hostel — to vast number of birds: there are waders all year round: turnstones; dunlin; purple sandpipers. Seabirds come here to breed: you may see cormorants and shags; gulls, kittiwakes and fulmars; eider ducks and terns; guillemots, razor-bills and little auks, plus thousands of puffins. There are ringed plover, oyster-catchers and rock pipits each year, plus occasional pairs of other birds. In addition hundreds of <u>kinds</u> of bird pass through here each year during migration.

The islands have been a bird sanctuary for over 100 years, but long before that St. Cuthbert had a special affection for eiders, that are still known on this coast as "Cuddy's ducks"

Seals colonise the islands, and can be seen curiously inspecting the passing boat-loads of people. In November the pups are born, mainly on the Wamses and the northern Hares (north of Longstone). Within a few weeks the young seals are weaned, and scattered across the northern oceans.

Rabbits also breed on the islands, and compete for burrow-space with the puffins.

Casual visitors are allowed to land only on Inner Farne. A landing fee is payable to the National Trust. The chapel may be visited: hermits and monks lived on the island during a period of nearly 900 years. Most remembered of them is St. Cuthbert, the holy man whose influence affected the church in Northern Britain for some centuries, and whose tomb is in a place of honour in Durham Cathedral.

- Boat-trips round the islands can be had (in suitable weather) from Seahouses. Take the landing fee for Inner Farne, binoculars, a good bird-book and warm clothing!

57.

The Farne Islands

The boat-landing, Inner Farne.

- Boat trips from Seahouses take you round the islands, giving you close views of the nesting and roosting birds, and the seals if there. A brief landing is usually on the itinerary – on Inner Farne of course. You can visit the chapel and walk round the island.

Cormorants on Staple Island

The Farne Islands

- Longstone sports the red and white lighthouse. From here Grace Darling set out with her father to row to the wreck on Big Harcar — in a storm!

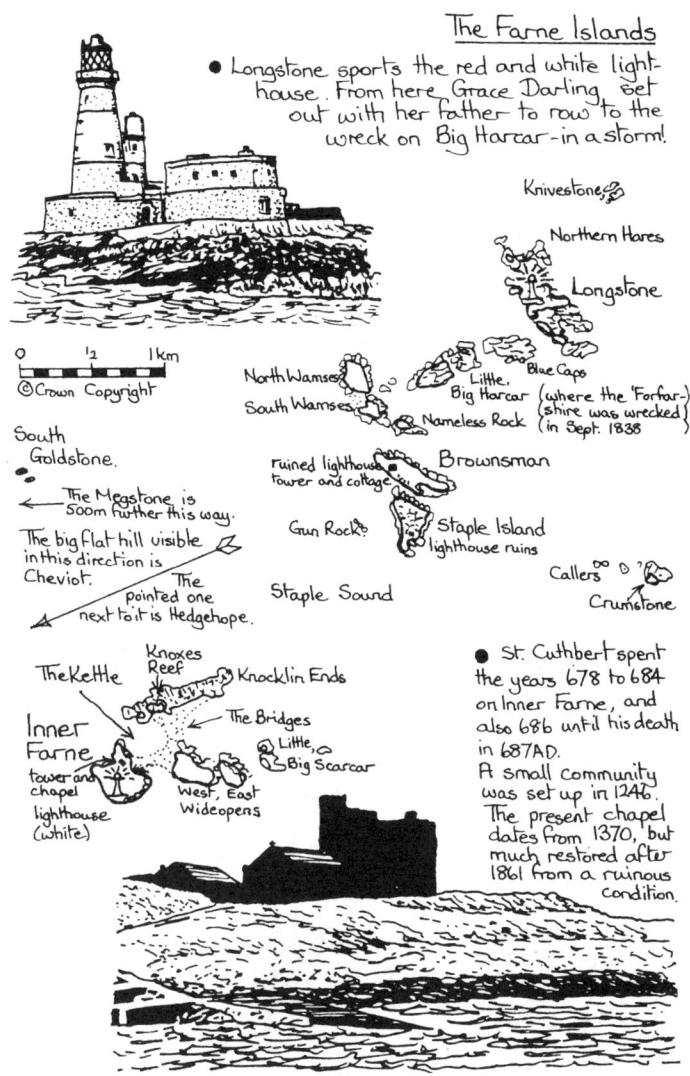

0   ½   1km
© Crown Copyright

Knivestone

Northern Hares

Longstone

North Wamses
South Wamses

Little, Big Harcar   Blue Caps
Nameless Rock   (where the 'Forfarshire' was wrecked in Sept. 1838)

South Goldstone.

← The Megstone is 500m further this way.

The big flat hill visible in this direction is Cheviot. The pointed one next to it is Hedgehope.

ruined lighthouse tower and cottage

Brownsman

Gun Rock   Staple Island lighthouse ruins

Staple Sound

Callers
Crumstone

The Kettle   Knoxes Reef   Knocklin Ends

Inner Farne
tower and chapel
lighthouse
(white)

The Bridges
Little, Big Scarcar
West, East Wideopens

- St. Cuthbert spent the years 678 to 684 on Inner Farne, and also 686 until his death in 687AD.
A small community was set up in 1246. The present chapel dates from 1370, but much restored after 1861 from a ruinous condition.

Seahouses to Beadnell. 4.7km (3 miles).

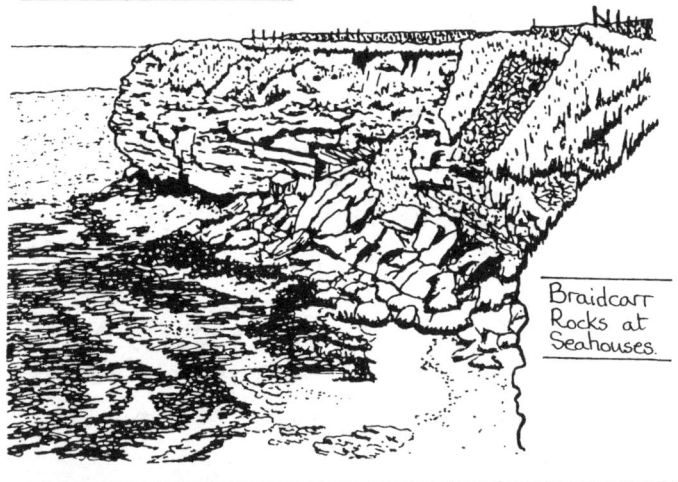

Braidcarr Rocks at Seahouses.

Beadnell Haven

Seahouses to Beadnell

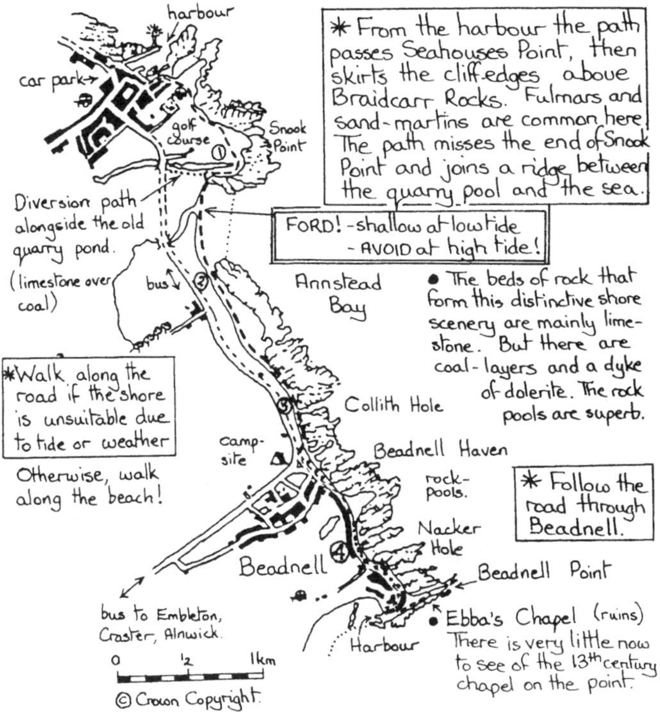

harbour
car park
golf course
Snook Point

* From the harbour the path passes Seahouses Point, then skirts the cliff-edges above Braidcarr Rocks. Fulmars and sand-martins are common here. The path misses the end of Snook Point and joins a ridge between the quarry pool and the sea.

Diversion path alongside the old quarry pond. (limestone over coal)

bus

FORD! – shallow at low tide – AVOID at high tide!

Annstead Bay

• The beds of rock that form this distinctive shore scenery are mainly limestone. But there are coal-layers and a dyke of dolerite. The rock pools are superb.

Collith Hole

*Walk along the road if the shore is unsuitable due to tide or weather. Otherwise, walk along the beach!

campsite

Beadnell Haven
rock-pools
Nacker Hole

* Follow the road through Beadnell.

Beadnell

Beadnell Point

bus to Embleton, Craster, Alnwick.

0 ½ 1km
© Crown Copyright.

Harbour
• Ebba's Chapel (ruins)
There is very little now to see of the 13th century chapel on the point.

Beadnell Point

61.

Beadnell

- Beadnell has two centres: the minuscule harbour and the old village.

- The <u>village</u>, missed by many heading for the harbour, has a fine church in its green heart. <u>St Ebba's</u> is a Victorian reconstruction of a 17th century church, with an unusual Gothic screen round the base of the spire.
Nearby is the <u>Craster Arms</u>, worth a look (as well as a visit). It incorporates <u>Beadnell Tower</u>, still with its 2½ metre-thick walls, and with the vaulted basement in use as a beer cellar.
The village also has a post office, shops, cafés and other hostelries. There is a camp-site and several caravansites.

- <u>St. Ebba's Chapel</u>, out on Beadnell Point (Ebba's Snook), is now little more than humps in the grass. A path goes to it from behind the limekilns.

Beadnell

- Beadnell's <u>limekilns</u>, by the harbour, are 18th century. Now they are looked after by the National Trust, and regarded as picturesque. But imagine them in use, belching foul smoke!
- The <u>harbour</u> is tiny but defended by massive walls. It is usually occupied by local <u>cobles</u> — the flat-bottomed, deep-prowed fishing boats of the North East of England.
The many yachts perch untidily on the magnificent beach.

Beadnell to Newton Haven   5.3km, (3¼ miles)

Beadnell Harbour from the south.

Football Hole

- Football Hole is a delight. A sandy sweep of beach in between rocky headlands. Smooth rounded dolerite boulders. A turquoise sea. Sit and watch the birds. Enjoy the flowers. Sunbathe. Forget the rest of the world — this is idyllic.

Low Newton

Beadnell to Newton Haven

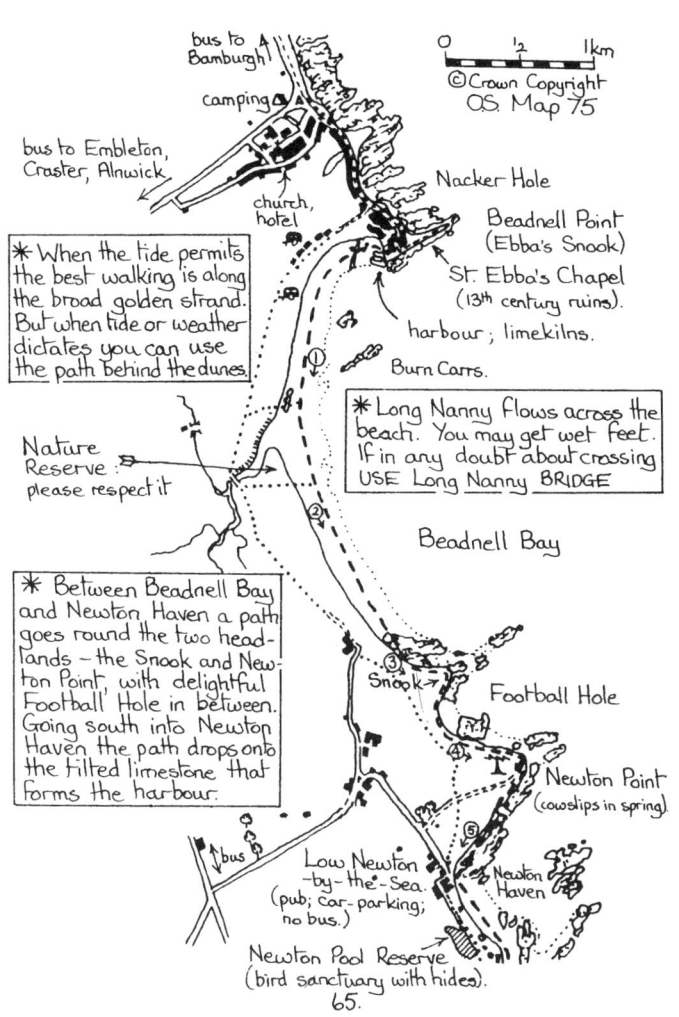

Low Newton-by-the-Sea to Embleton 2.8km (1¾ miles)

Embleton Bay: the view to Dunstanburgh Castle from Low Newton-by-the-Sea

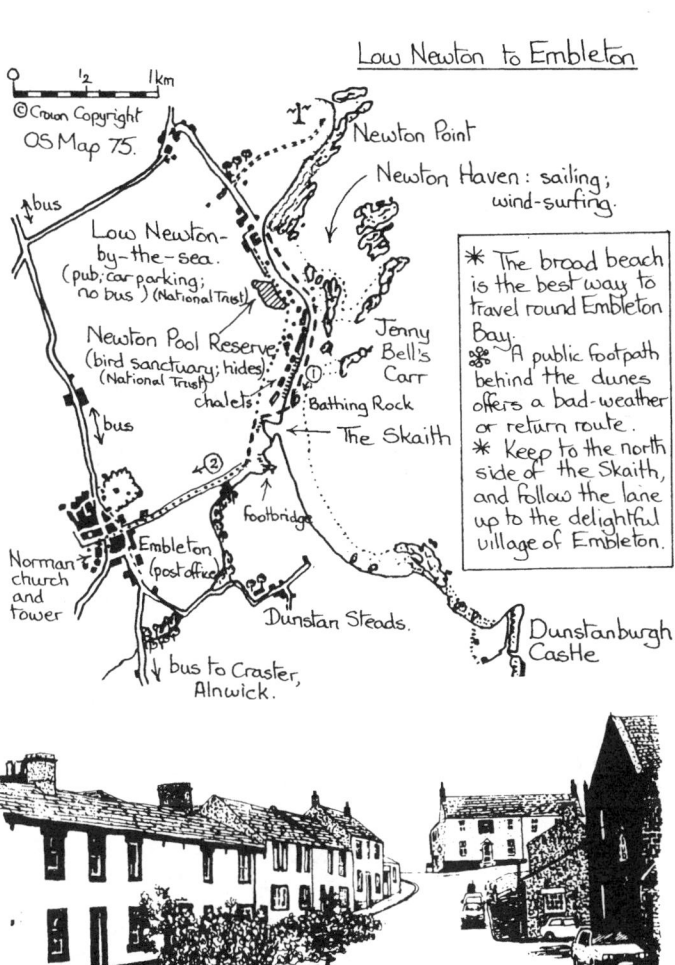

Low Newton to Embleton

- Newton Point
- Newton Haven: sailing; wind-surfing.
- Low Newton-by-the-sea. (pub; car parking; no bus) (National Trust)
- Newton Pool Reserve (bird sanctuary; hides) (National Trust)
- chalets
- Jenny Bell's Carr
- Bathing Rock
- The Skaith
- footbridge
- Embleton (post office)
- Norman church and tower
- Dunstan Steads.
- Dunstanburgh Castle
- bus to Craster, Alnwick.

* The broad beach is the best way to travel round Embleton Bay.
* A public footpath behind the dunes offers a bad-weather or return route.
* Keep to the north side of the Skaith, and follow the lane up to the delightful village of Embleton.

© Crown Copyright OS Map 75.

Embleton

Embleton

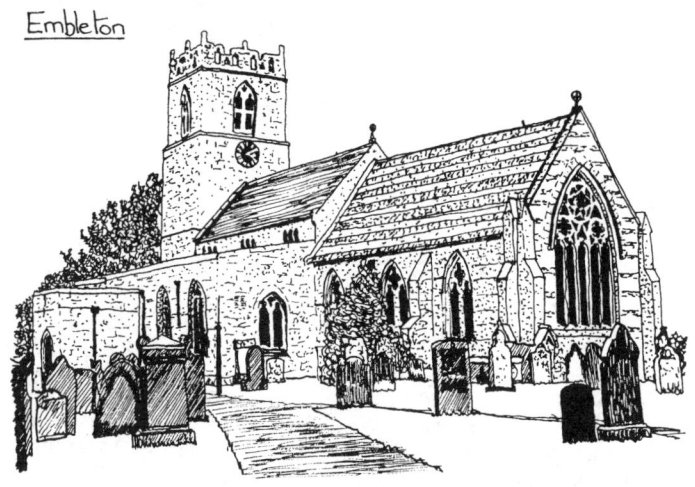

- **Embleton** is an attractive little village with a cluster of houses rising up the bank beside the triangular green. This sports a pump and a pant as well as a telephone box. More of the village is scattered round a larger square plan. There are churches and inns, a post-office and shops. At the south-west corner is <u>Holy Trinity Church</u>. This looks like a typical Victorian building, but go inside, where its ancient bones are revealed, dating back in the base of the tower to about 1200 AD. Read its history, and ponder why the chancel is fitted at an odd angle! Beside the church, but private, is the <u>Vicar's Tower</u>. This was built in 1395, and incorporated later into the more comfortable vicarage.

3.5 km (2¼ miles)   Embleton to Dunstanburgh Castle.

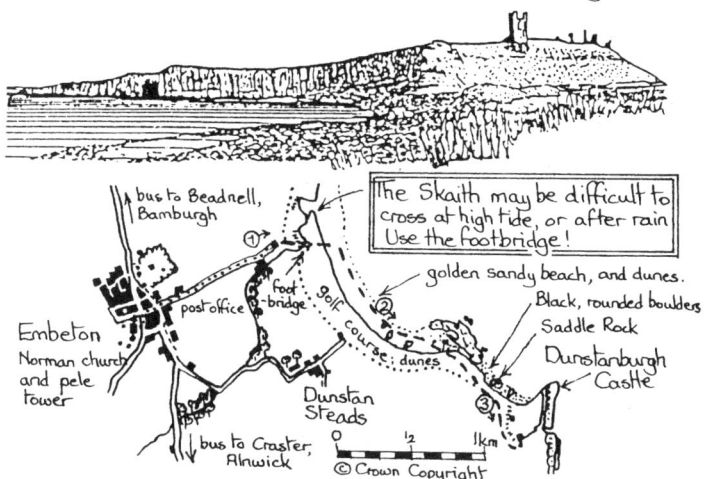

The Skaith may be difficult to cross at high tide, or after rain. Use the footbridge!

* Walk up the hill past the green in the village, and on along the lane that descends to Embleton Links. Cross the Skaith by the footbridge and walk along the glorious beach to the south-east. When the beach becomes bouldery the path goes on across the grass behind, skirting round under the walls of Dunstanburgh Castle.
Do NOT attempt to walk round the Dunstanburgh headland at sea-level! But do use binoculars to observe the birds that nest or roost on the dramatic black cliffs.

❋ The path behind the dunes provides a high-tide or return route.

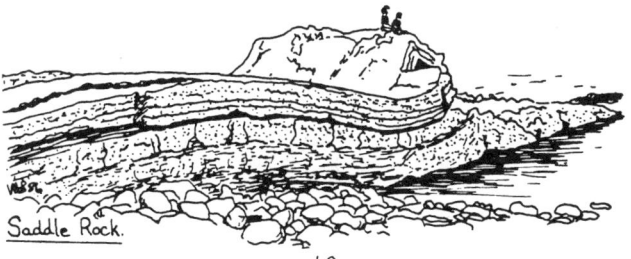

Saddle Rock.

Dunstanburgh Castle

Lilburn Tower

- Despite its grandeur and its impressive location, Dunstanburgh Castle has played only a brief and minor rôle in national events. It was built late. Thomas, Earl of Lancaster had it built as a secure refuge, starting in 1313 (he was executed for treason in 1322). Sir John Lilburn became constable, and had the Lilburn Tower built, around 1325. John of Gaunt, when Lieutenant of the Scottish Marches built another gateway in about 1380, the massive gatehouse being walled up as a keep.

During the Wars of the Roses the castle changed hands several times. Queen Margaret is reputed to have stayed here after the Battle of Hexham before taking ship from the cove below. But the development of artillery rendered the castle redundant, and from 1464, after only 140 years use, the castle fell into disrepair. By 1550 it was considered a ruin.

It is a remarkable tribute to its builders that so much remains standing after 500 years of neglect. Now it is in the hands of English Heritage, who charge an admission fee and have useful guides to the castle and its wildlife. They also have postcards!

Dunstanburgh Castle

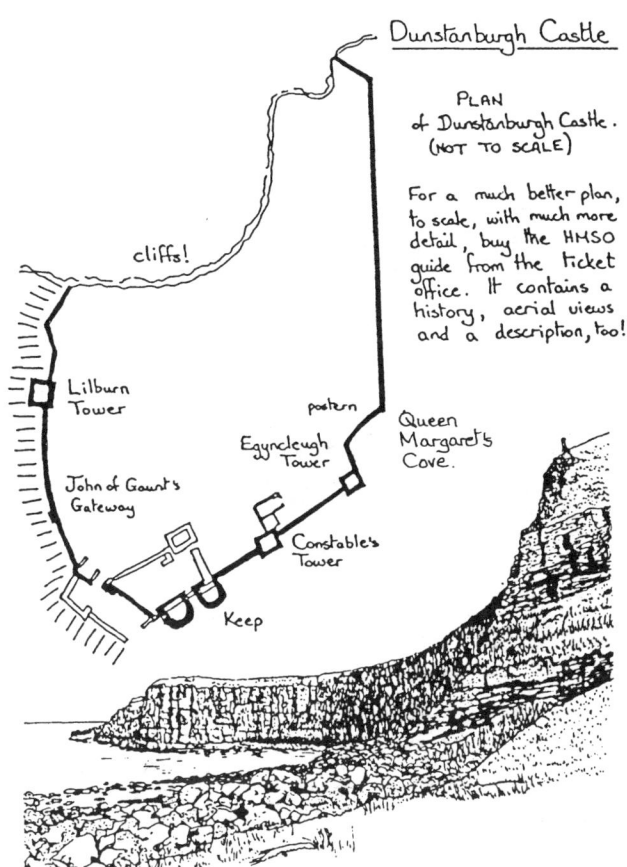

PLAN of Dunstanburgh Castle. (NOT TO SCALE)

For a much better plan, to scale, with much more detail, buy the HMSO guide from the ticket office. It contains a history, aerial views and a description, too!

- The designers of the castle selected a site that offers superb natural protection. The great Bailey occupies the top of an outcrop of the Great Whin Sill. (This is the basalt that appears throughout Northumbria: High Force tumbles down over it; Hadrian's Wall strides along it; Bamburgh and Dunstanburgh Castles perch atop it.) As a result, no walls at all are required on the north side.

Dunstanburgh

The Keep.

* From the Castle gate follow the track southwards, gently descending towards the rocky promontory of Cushat Stiel. Continue on the path as it veers right, dropping down through a rim of rocks to pass the little bay of Nova Scotia. Now you can walk on fine turf all the way to Craster, or you could digress onto the rocky foreshore.

John of Gaunt's Gateway — Lilburn Tower — The Keep (original gate) — Constable's Tower — Egyncleugh Tower

2.0km (1¼ miles).   ## Dunstanburgh Castle to Craster

✤ If you are walking from Craster to the castle, and then back, the path over the heughs may provide an interesting diversion: The path passes through the Shaird, a gap in the low hills (heughs), then follows the foot of the whinstone cliff. Gorse, bracken, bluebells and hawthorn feature strongly in their seasons.

Map labels: Dunstanburgh Castle; Queen Margaret's Cove; Nova Scotia – the wreck of a trawler may be seen; Scrog Hill; The Shaird; The Heughs; Dunstan Square; bus to Embleton, Beadnell, Bamburgh...; narrow arched gateway; harbour; Craster Tower

The path is on close-cropped turf, grazed by friendly cows.

The rocky shore is dotted with pools.

0   ½   1km
© Crown Copyright
O.S. Maps 75, 81

- <u>Craster Tower</u> has been the family seat of the Craster family since 1272. The tower itself dates from before 1415.

Information Centre, **Nature Reserve** and car-park.

- <u>Craster</u> lies in a natural hollow between the heughs, that afford it shelter from north and south (unlike most villages on the Northumberland coast, that have exposed locations).
  The natural harbour is reinforced by two massive jetties. Whinstone from the quarry used to be exported from here.
  Fishing cobles still venture out for lobsters and herring. Kippers are a Craster speciality, with a wide reputation.
  Buses for both coastal directions come into the village to turn round. Car-parking is available (for a small fee) at the quarry, where there is also a purpose-built information Centre and a Nature Reserve.

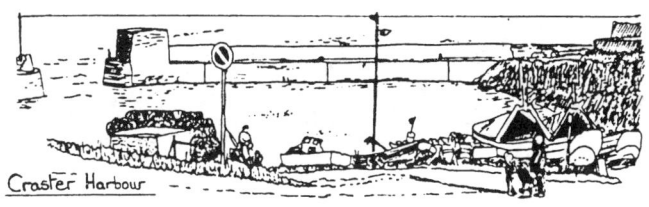

Craster Harbour

Craster to Howick.

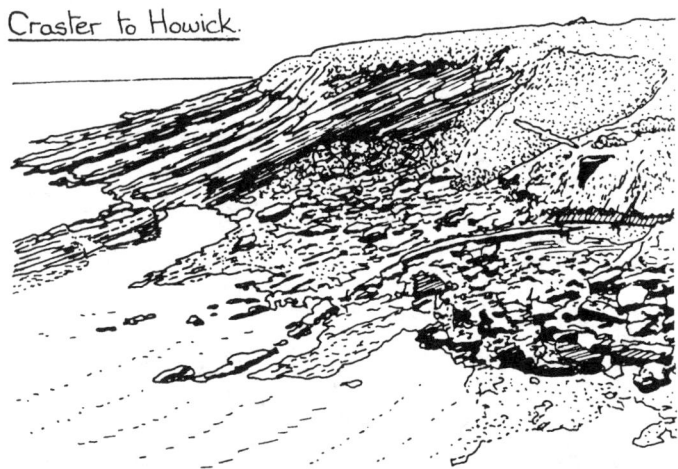

- South of Craster the raw bones of the land lie exposed: Long Heugh, ending in Cullernose Point, is of dolerite, hard & columnar. Swine Den, the little bay south of the point, is floored with round whinstone boulders. Next come great folds of grey limestone, arched and twisted by geological pressures. Yellow sandstones make up the cliffs beyond. Explore the beach and look at the fascinating skeleton of strata revealed.

Craster to Howick.

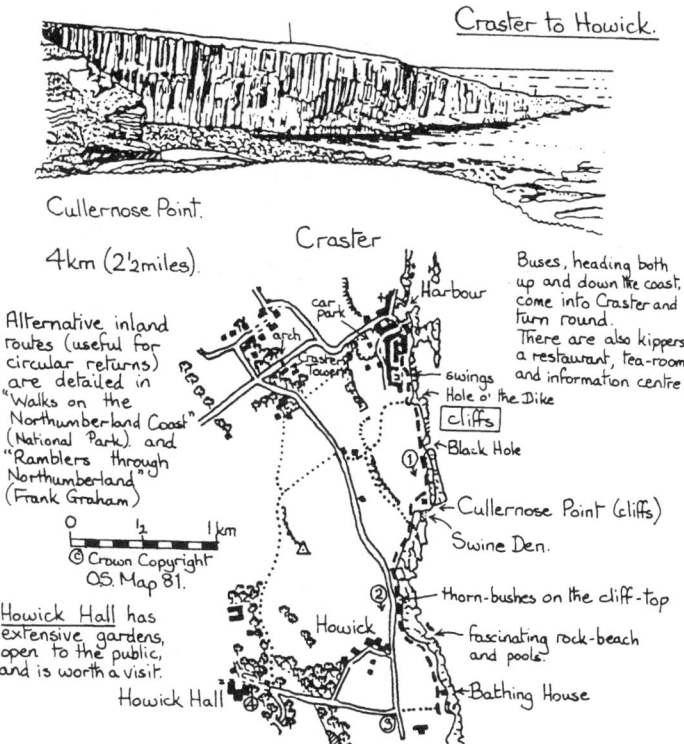

Cullernose Point.

4km (2½ miles).

Alternative inland routes (useful for circular returns) are detailed in "Walks on the Northumberland Coast" (National Park) and "Ramblers through Northumberland" (Frank Graham)

© Crown Copyright OS. Map 81.

- Howick Hall has extensive gardens, open to the public, and is worth a visit.

Buses, heading both up and down the coast, come into Craster and turn round.
There are also kippers, a restaurant, tea-room, and information centre.

Cullernose Point (cliffs)
Swine Den.
thorn-bushes on the cliff-top
fascinating rock-beach and pools
Bathing House

*The coast-walk leaves Craster beyond the children's play-park. Follow the cliff past the school, then jink abruptly round Hole o' the Dyke and continue along the cliffs. Pass the sinister-sounding Black Hole to the heights of Cullernose Point. When the tide is out, the view is spectacular, revealing the strata of rock that underlie the bay to the south. Turn down to the west, and follow the path south. Look back at the face of the cliffs, and note the smoothly folded limestone closer to hand. The path climbs up to meet the narrow lane. Thorn bushes, with paths half-buried in them, occupy the space between lane and cliff. After a few hundred metres or so the path veers off to follow the cliffs again. Now these are negotiable in places, so that with care you can pick a grassy route down to the beach, if you wish to look at the rocks, picnic, sunbathe.... The path continues along the top to the bathing-house near Rumbling Kern.

Howick Hall

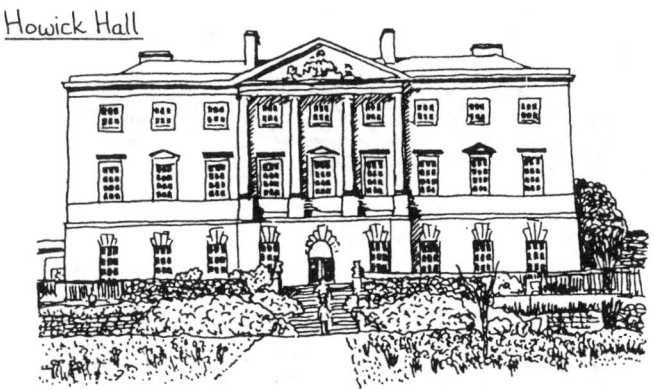

- <u>Howick Hall</u> is the home of the Grey family. The Hall was built in 1782 to a design by William Newton of Newcastle, on a site that had been occupied by a tower since before 1416. Just across the burn to the south is the <u>church</u>, dating from 1746. The <u>gardens</u> are extensive, attractive and informative. They are open to the public on spring and summer afternoons. A visit when the grounds are swathed in daffodils, with the first rhododendrons bursting into bloom and the buds breaking on the trees, will never be forgotten. The <u>Silver Wood</u> is a marvelous woodland of beech with elms and conifers. A <u>woodland walk</u> crosses the public road by a bridge, and continues down beside Howick Burn to the sea. Behind the beach the woods are carpeted with unusual double-bloom daffodils.

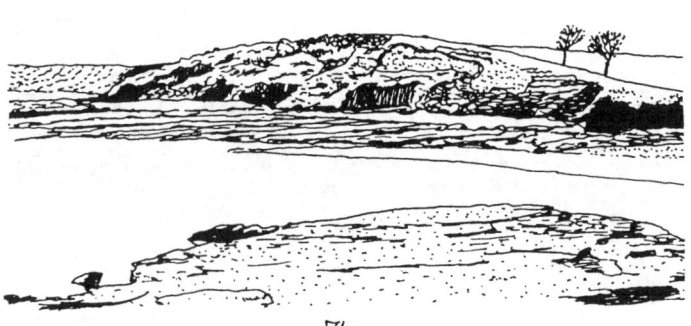

Howick Hall

Howick to Boulmer

• Rumbling Kern is just south of the bathing house. It is a large hole in the rocks, through which the sea sucks and surges. There are superb sheltered spots on the beaches and rocks. Enjoy the rock-pools, and the interesting rock formations.

* From the bathing house there is a choice of routes to the bridge over Howick Burn: — the beach is best, if the tide permits; — the cliff path is badly eroded and is not recommended;
* a sign-posted alternative route goes inland to the road corner, then south to reach the footbridge.
* The route continues either along the shore or the cliff-path above. There is a succession of delightful bays and magnificent rocks, all the way to Boulmer.

Part of boiler from the French trawler 'Tadorne'

5km, (3 miles)

Howick to Boulmer

The bathing house at Howick.

Howick Hall (The gardens and woodland walk to the sea are private. The public is admitted during spring and summer afternoons, for a small fee).

- **The bathing house** was built for the Grey family in Victorian times. Just below it is a rectangular pool, with iron hooks and socket holes in the rock, presumably for tents or awnings.

- **RAF Boulmer** is the base for the Rescue helicopters.

Map labels:
- buses to Craster
- bathing house
- Howick Seahouses
- Rumbling Kern
- Howick Haven
- mineral springs in cliffs
- bridge over road
- crumbly cliffs
- part of wrecked ship's boiler
- bridge
- Iron Scars
- Sugar Sands
- buses to Alnwick
- primroses and cowslips
- Howdiemont Sands
- Longhoughton Steel
- car park
- Boulmer
- Bewick Stone
- 'Fishing Boat'
- toilets
- Life-boat station
- Post Office
- infrequent buses to Alnmouth, Alnwick
- bus shelter
- Boulmer Haven

© Crown Copyright

79.

Boulmer

- Boulmer has a long tradition of smuggling. Some of the houses are reputed to have hidden cellars, once used for caching rum and other contraband. The 'Fishing Boat' Inn has been associated with the 'free trade'.

The Haven is almost enclosed by a ring of rocks, that break up the seas that pound the coast. The narrow gap to provide access is marked from the shore by the two leading marks (right).

Boulmer also has a tradition of life-saving. A lifeboat was maintained here between 1825 and 1968, with a long list of rescues along this wild coast. Since the RNLI departed, the Boulmer Volunteer Rescue Service has continued, using the old lifeboat station (right, below), next to the Coastguard equipment store and the diminutive post office (below).

6 km, (3¾ miles)

Boulmer to Alnmouth

* From Boulmer take the track opposite the tiny Post Office, across the grassy back-shore to the beach. Here, behind the Haven, the shore is striped with lines of shells, periwinkles and limpets mainly, but some razor-shells too. A large patch of dolerite boulders litters the beach, that gives way to sandstone slabs as Seaton Point is approached....

0 ½ 1 km
© Crown Copyright
OS Map 81.

labels on map: 'Fishing Boat' Inn, toilets, Volunteer lifeboat, Post Office, Boulmer Haven, bus shelter, leading lights, coastguard lookout + mast, Marmouth Scars, Seaton Point, infrequent buses, Foxton Hall, golf course, Marden House, R. Aln, ridge, golf course, old lifeboat house, golf course, sand, toilets, Church Hill, Marden Rocks.

* Round Seaton Point keep to the belt of sand or to the slabs of rock, if possible. Watch for brittle-stars (a delicate star-fish) Follow the sandy beach past Foxton Hall — now the club-house for the golf-course.

* Either continue along the broad sandy beach to the mouth of the Aln, or climb up a footpath to a derelict cottage (Marden House), and follow the fence and wall up onto the splendid ridge. You have earned a sit on one of the seats, so enjoy the view south, to Warkworth, Amble, Coquet Island.....

Pony rides on Alnmouth Beach.

81.

Alnmouth

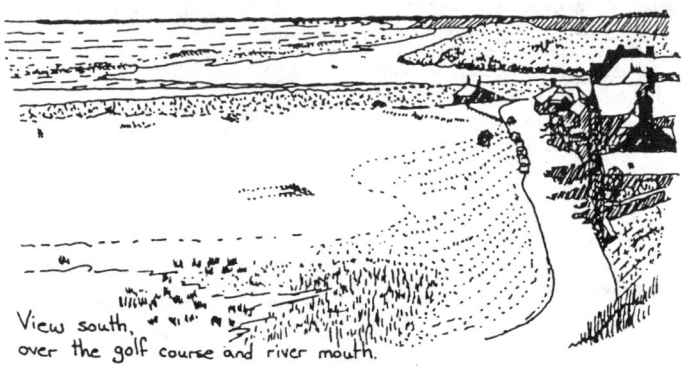

View south, over the golf course and river mouth.

- <u>Alnmouth</u> is a quiet residential town, with a genteel holiday trade that is catered for by a number of hotels and guest houses. There are sheltered moorings for small craft, a golf course and magnificent beaches. The main street boasts several shops and places to eat. One little window onto the street holds a reminder of the town's former economic importance as a port: a barometric station, courtesy of a Duke of Northumberland.
- At the top of the town there is a <u>Franciscan Friary</u>. The friars have a superb view southwards along the golden coastline to Amble, Hauxley and Coquet Island. Even the "Nine Men of Lynemouth" can be seen on a good day.

Alnmouth seen from Church Hill.

Alnmouth

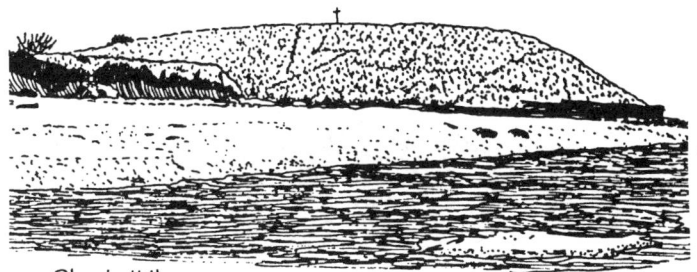

Church Hill

- The tall buildings that give Alnmouth much of its character owe their origins to the granaries of the mediaeval port. This was an important grain port then. But the shipping has gone, and the town has changed its function. There are no quays now. Even the river has changed its course. A great storm in 1806 cut a new channel to the sea, separating Church Hill from the rest of the town. The storm also wrecked the Norman church on the hill. A new church was built in the town, and the ruins on Church Hill crumbled away. Only a few foundations of the even more ancient Saxon church of St. Waleric remain. The harbour silted up, dunes covered the old river mouth, and the harbour buildings disappeared (except for a ruinous chapel).

The present town is quite well served by public transport, with frequent buses to Alnwick, and south to Warkworth and Newcastle. Occasional buses operate to Boulmer.

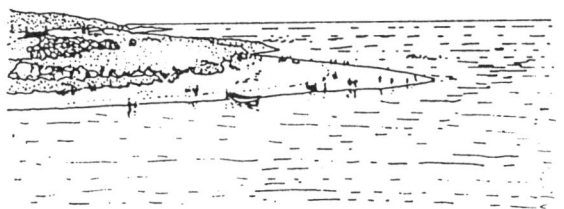

<u>Alnmouth to Alnmouth Station.</u>   3.4km (2 miles).

- The Aln winds down from <u>Lesbury</u>; seen from the Alnmouth-Boulmer road.

- <u>Lesbury Church</u> dates from Norman times. The tower and chancel are 13th century.

- <u>Lesbury</u>: quiet suburbia; hedges, gardens and magnificent trees.

Alnmouth to Alnmouth Station.

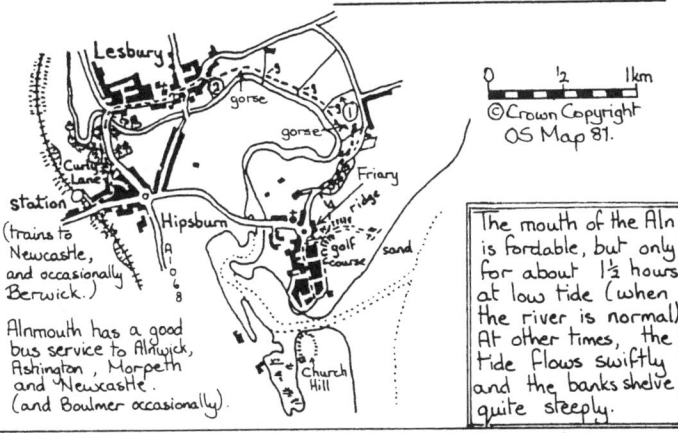

© Crown Copyright
OS Map 81.

(trains to Newcastle, and occasionally Berwick.)

Alnmouth has a good bus service to Alnwick, Ashington, Morpeth and Newcastle. (and Boulmer occasionally).

The mouth of the Aln is fordable, but only for about 1½ hours at low tide (when the river is normal) At other times, the tide flows swiftly and the banks shelve quite steeply.

The quickest way from Alnmouth to the station, on foot, is straight up the main road. But if you have time, go along by the river.
If you have not already climbed up onto the ridge beside the Friary, do so, and enjoy the view south. Take the path beside the Friary, close to the trig. point and descend steeply by the edge of the wood. (If you have already been up the hill you can cheat by walking up the lane from the roundabout at the top of Alnmouth). As you follow the lane past the wood the hedge on the left drops away. Follow a descending path down and across the fields by the river.

As you approach Lesbury the path disappears near a gorse patch. Rise up across the field, and carefully locate the way out of the field: a narrow way between a bungalow and its garage, with a sign-post at the road-end.

Follow the road through Lesbury. The east end is pleasantly suburban, much influenced by the presence of RAF Boulmer, with its massive radar installations. Pass the church and continue through the older part of the village, with its golden sand-stone and beautiful trees.

At the main road, turn down to the old bridge, still carrying the main A1068 road. Cross carefully. On the south side, the wall beside the road is all that remains of a farm-house. Beyond, the footpath is segregated from the narrow road, behind a hedge of magnificent trees. At a road junction, bear right up the aptly-named Curly Lane, that delivers you to the head of the station approach.

Alnmouth Station to Warkworth Beach 7.9 km (5 miles).

• The rescue helicopter from RAF Boulmer — the "bionic budgie" is a frequent sight as it makes sorties up and down the coastline.
Give the crew a friendly wave: it may make their day!

North of Birling Carrs, looking north towards Alnmouth.

The path towards Warkworth.

Alnmouth Station to Warkworth Beach.

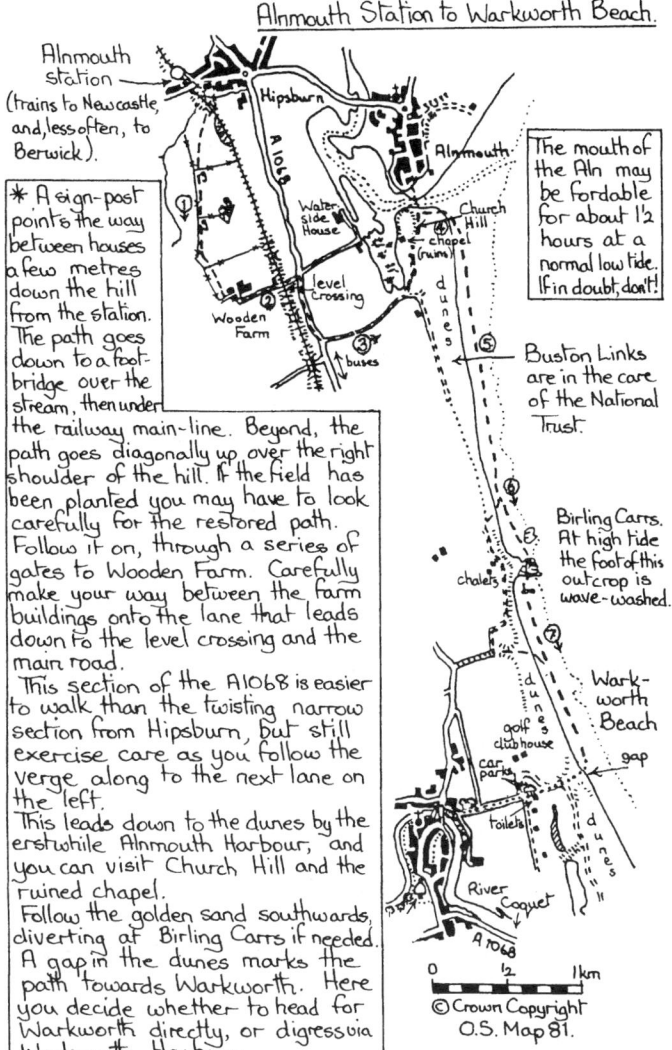

Alnmouth station (trains to Newcastle and, less often, to Berwick).

*A sign-post points the way between houses a few metres down the hill from the station. The path goes down to a foot-bridge over the stream, then under the railway main-line. Beyond, the path goes diagonally up over the right shoulder of the hill. If the field has been planted you may have to look carefully for the restored path. Follow it on, through a series of gates to Wooden Farm. Carefully make your way between the farm buildings onto the lane that leads down to the level crossing and the main road.

This section of the A1068 is easier to walk than the twisting narrow section from Hipsburn, but still exercise care as you follow the verge along to the next lane on the left.

This leads down to the dunes by the erstwhile Alnmouth Harbour, and you can visit Church Hill and the ruined chapel.

Follow the golden sand southwards, diverting at Birling Carrs if needed. A gap in the dunes marks the path towards Warkworth. Here you decide whether to head for Warkworth directly, or digress via Warkworth Harbour.

The mouth of the Aln may be fordable for about 1½ hours at a normal low tide. If in doubt, don't!

Buston Links are in the care of the National Trust.

Birling Carrs. At high tide the foot of this outcrop is wave-washed.

Warkworth Beach

0   ½   1km

© Crown Copyright
O.S. Map 81.

87.

Warkworth: beach to harbour to town. 6km (3¾ miles)

* Continue south-eastwards along the strand of fine sand, to reach the North Pier at the mouth of the River Coquet. You may wish to venture out on the pier, but do note the warning signs.
The track beside the old harbour is not a right of way, but does provide a convenient return route. It may be flooded! The little tower that you can see to the west is the topmost lookout on top of Warkworth's Castle keep.
The track — built for pier repair traffic — turns left. A path goes up steps, past toilets and a carpark, then joins the lane leading across to Warkworth. This descends to meet the main road just by the bridges at the north end of town. Cross into town by the Norman bridge, past the unusual bridge-tower.

• Until 1765 the Coquet performed a last loop before entering the sea — more or less at the gap in the dunes by the lane from Warkworth. Since then Warkworth Harbour has gradually silted up. Now its mud-flats are important for bird-life. The river was eventually tamed by the breakwaters (1836), rebuilt in the 1980s.

Warkworth: beach to harbour to town

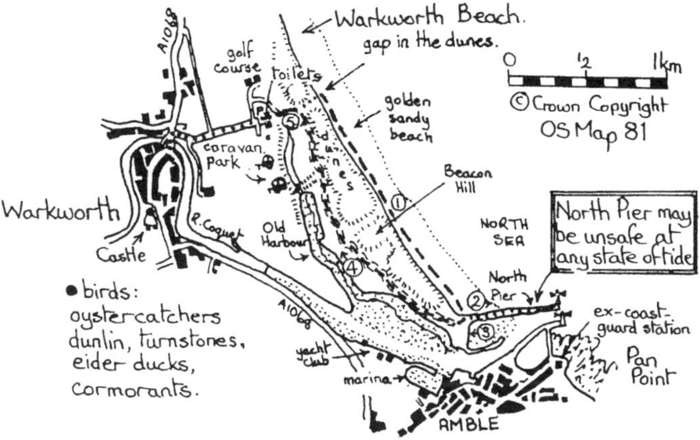

Map features labeled: Warkworth Beach, gap in the dunes, golf course, toilets, golden sandy beach, caravan park, Warkworth Castle, R. Coquet, Old Harbour, dunes, Beacon Hill, NORTH SEA, North Pier, ex-coastguard station, Pan Point, yacht club, marina, AMBLE, A1068

© Crown Copyright
OS Map 81

0 — ½ — 1 km

North Pier may be unsafe at any state of tide

- birds: oystercatchers, dunlin, turnstones, eider ducks, cormorants.

Over the bridge into Warkworth

ADVERTISEMENT: Warkworth is more fully described in "Warkworth" or "Alnwick, Morpeth, Rothbury and Warkworth."

89.

<u>Warkworth</u> must not be rushed, nor passed by. Here is one of Northumberland's treasures. The town sits in a loop of river, with the castle at the top of the street, so that the town is protected from all directions. Pause, and enjoy its offerings:

- The <u>Norman bridge</u> has a defensive tower, through which all traffic had to pass until 1965 (when the new bridge was built alongside). Few English towns have anything like this.

- The <u>Church of St. Lawrence</u>, by the river at the foot of the main street. This largely Norman church is built on Saxon remains. It is worth a visit. Respect it as a place of worship, not just as an antiquity. Not all visitors have shown respect: in 1174 the Scots massacred the men, women and children of the town, who had gathered in the church as refuge.

- The <u>riverside path</u> runs right round the town, becoming a lane on the eastern side. From the bridge it goes west past St. Lawrence, and on round the bend of river. It is a charming walk at any season. Here is the Coquet at its best, cloaked in beautiful trees. You should make time to follow the path upriver — come back to do it if necessary. You will reach a boat landing beneath the castle walls, where in summer you may be able to hire a rowing boat. Walk on up the path — or row upriver — for more romantic scenery: the castle looks down on this stretch through a frame of magnificent trees.

- The <u>Hermitage</u> lies upstream about a half-mile beyond the castle. It is on the north bank, and only accessible across the ferry from the riverside path. Here, carved into the rock, is a cell comprising chapel, confessional and dormitory. Various legends surround its purpose, but its real history is still obscure. It is in the care of English Heritage, like the castle.

- The <u>town</u> is a relatively unspoiled Northumberland village. The street runs down from the castle towards the church, then veers off to the bridge. There are some shops, public houses, tea-rooms and a post office. Buses run north to Alnmouth and Alnwick, south to Amble, Ashington, Newcastle.
Behind the frontages the gardens maintain the mediæval property patterns, running in long narrow strips (burgages) down from the street to the riverbank track. Those on the east side are bisected by the direct footpath between castle and bridge — another fascinating digression.

Warkworth

A winter evening in Warkworth: a view upstream from the bridge. Below: the Norman bridge itself, with a backcloth of spring trees.

Warkworth Castle

The castle dominates, over river and town.

Warkworth Castle

- The castle has been here, in some form, since at least 1139. Then Henry, son of the King of Scotland, was made Earl of Northumberland. Later the castle became the property of the Percy family. It was greatly strengthened. It was a bastion against the Scots and a symbol of national power too. This is the castle of Harry Hotspur, featuring in "Henry IV (part 1)" by Shakespeare.

  The castle declined during the Percy family's absence from Northumberland after their fall from favour, but they gave it their attention again in the 18th century, before finally choosing Alnwick to be the modern family seat.

  Now English Heritage is the castle custodian, and makes a charge for visits. They also publish an excellent detailed guide.

Warkworth to Amble. 3.5km (2.4 miles)

Warkworth Castle from the east

Amble: the yacht-moorings and marina development site (1987)

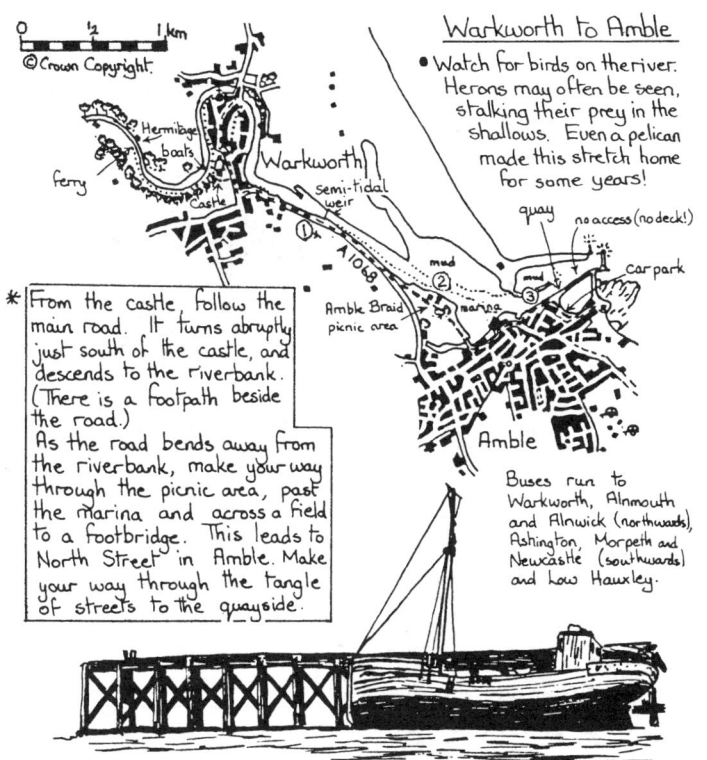

Warkworth to Amble

- Watch for birds on the river. Herons may often be seen, stalking their prey in the shallows. Even a pelican made this stretch home for some years!

> From the castle, follow the main road. It turns abruptly just south of the castle, and descends to the riverbank. (There is a footpath beside the road.)
> As the road bends away from the riverbank, make your way through the picnic area, past the marina and across a field to a footbridge. This leads to North Street in Amble. Make your way through the tangle of streets to the quayside.

Buses run to Warkworth, Alnmouth and Alnwick (northwards), Ashington, Morpeth and Newcastle (southwards) and Low Hauxley.

- <u>Amble</u> is a solidly-built, business-like town. It used to rely on the export of coal from its own pit (and others) that was brought down to the staithes by rail. You may notice the gaps in the town where the tracks came through, and the staithe, now without tracks or trucks.

Some grain is still shipped out, and some fish are still landed. But mainly Amble survives as a resort. There are golf links, a developing marina, fishing (from the pier and by boat) and marvellous sands stretching down the coast. It also caters for the residential, refreshment and entertainment needs of its visitors.

Amble

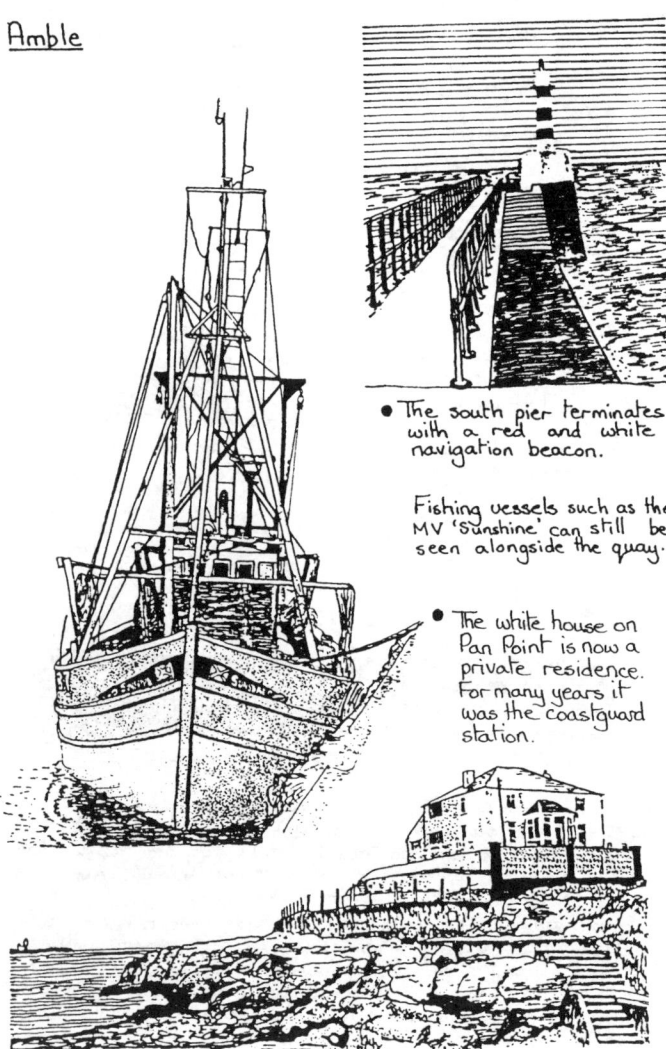

- The south pier terminates with a red and white navigation beacon.

Fishing vessels such as the MV 'Sunshine' can still be seen alongside the quay.

- The white house on Pan Point is now a private residence. For many years it was the coastguard station.

5.0km (3miles)   Amble to Hadston Carrs

- <u>Coquet Island</u> is famous as the abode of Cuthbert, the Northumbrian saint, who occupied the Benedictine Cell on the island as a hermit, until persuaded to accept the bishopric by the abbess of Whitby, Elfreda, when she visited the isle in AD 684. Other hermits have lived here too: St. Henry of Coquet was a Dane who dwelt here in the 11th century. The Scots captured it in 1645 despite a large garrison of 200 men.

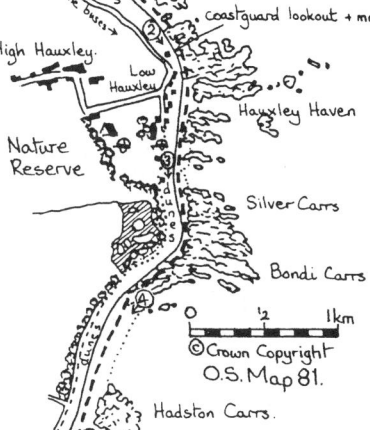

* From the quayside in Amble follow the edge of the pool round to Pan Point. Cross this inland of the erstwhile coastguard station (now a private residence). Descend to the rocky beach if possible, and follow it south round Hauxley Point.
* Alternatively, pick a route along the dunes or even along the quiet road to Low Hauxley, and the footpath beyond.

97.

Druridge Bay.

View south towards Cresswell and Lynemouth.

Looking north along the dunes, towards Hauxley and Coquet Island.

5.2km (3¼miles).   # Hadston Carrs to Druridge

- <u>Druridge Bay</u> stretches between Hauxley and Cresswell, seven miles of broad sandy beach, backed by dunes. Looking north, it appears to end with a light-house, but that is on Coquet Island, not the mainland. Southwards, the bay ends at Snab Point, but the eye is drawn onwards to the tall chimneys of Lynemouth.

- Behind the dunes, the <u>Country Park</u> has been reclaimed from the open-cast mining that has ravaged this part of Northumberland. In 1970 the park was started, but suffered a set-back when the lake broke through into old workings underground, in 1974. In 1982-3 the lake bed was re-lined with clay (from an adjacent open-cast site) and the lake was refilled. Trees planted in the 70's are coming to form a positive feature of the landscape in the 90's

- The <u>beach</u> is seldom totally deserted. Even in mid-winter there are occasional joggers, horse-riders, dog-walkers, bikers, beach-combers and even walkers. In summer it can be a marvelous place to sun-bathe in seclusion: people can spread out a long way with seven miles of sand and dunes.

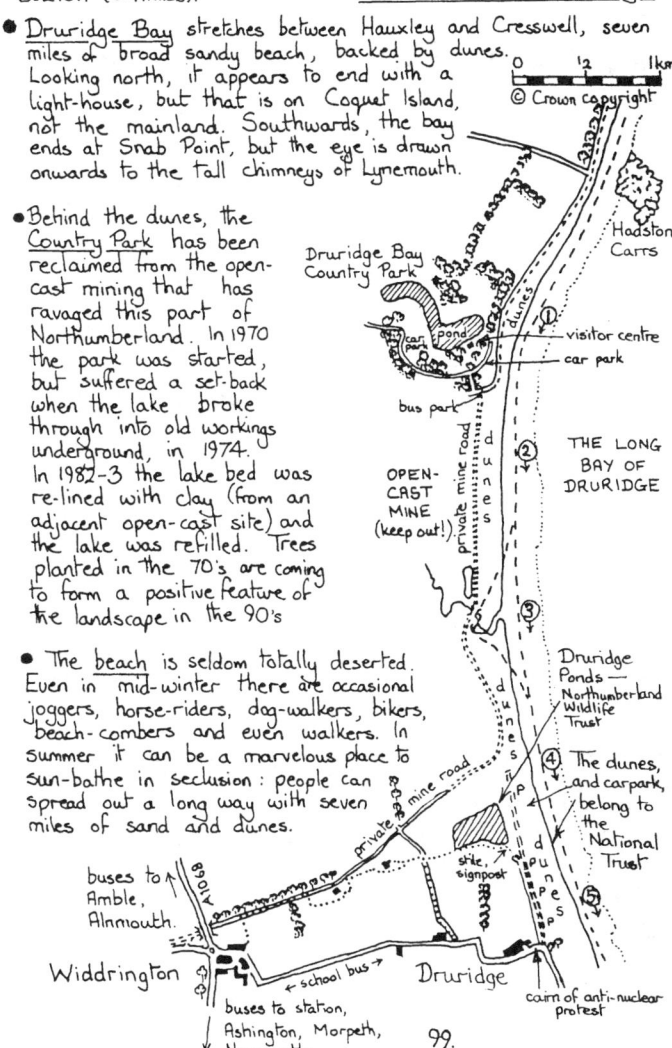

99.

Druridge to Cresswell 2.9km (1¾ miles)

Blakemoor Pool.

Whether you are walking along the beach or the road this is a large landscape: the great long curve of golden sand, backed by dunes, or flat farmland stretching away to the horizon. Only the chimneys of Lynemouth - the Nine Men - visible on the southern skyline give a hint of industry. Yet this rural scene has been an industrial battleground, on two fronts.

Most long-standing has been the protest about extraction of sand from the beach by Government-granted licence. It seems like a sound idea: you dig out sand from a hole in the beach, and the sea refills it! But that sand comes from somewhere, and the conservators of the magnificent dunes (the National Trust and Northumberland County Council) have cause for concern.

Druridge was also proposed as a site for a nuclear power station, despite Northumberland's massive coal-field. This proposal is in the background at present, since Chernobyl and a re-evaluation of nuclear power economics made even Governments reconsider the nuclear option.

Cresswell from Snab Point.

Druridge to Cresswell

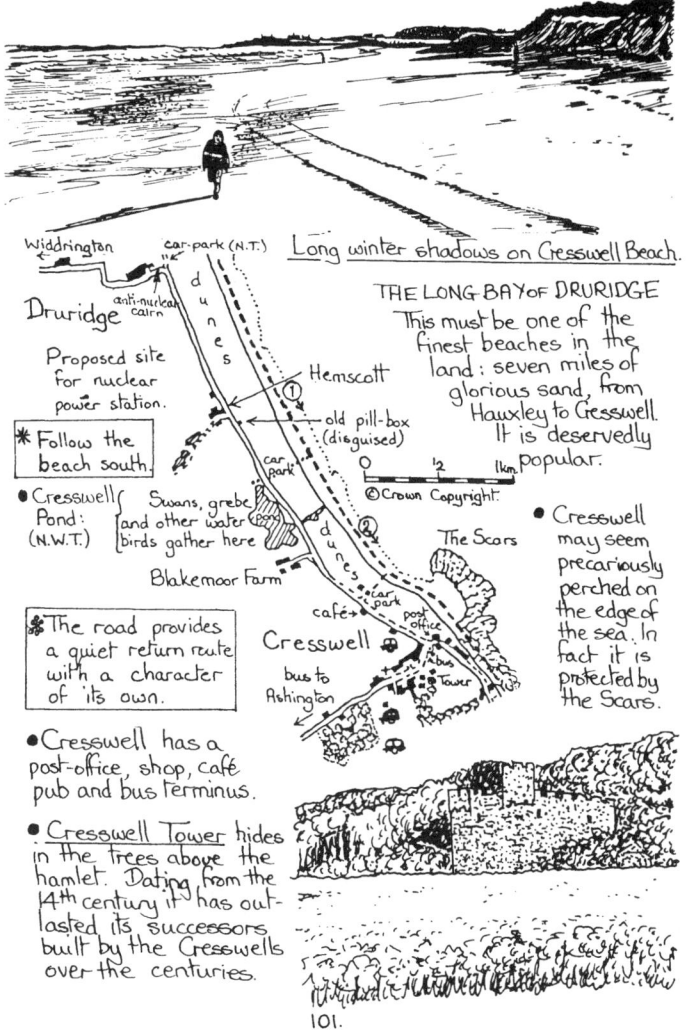

Long winter shadows on Cresswell Beach.

Druridge — Widdington, car-park (N.T.)

Proposed site for nuclear power station.

※ **Follow the beach south.**

• Cresswell Pond: (N.W.T.)

Swans, grebe and other water birds gather here

Blakemoor Farm

THE LONG BAY OF DRURIDGE

This must be one of the finest beaches in the land: seven miles of glorious sand, from Hauxley to Cresswell. It is deservedly popular.

Hemscott — old pill-box (disguised) — car park — dunes

© Crown Copyright.

The Scars — car park — post office — Cresswell — café — bus to Ashington — Tower

• Cresswell may seem precariously perched on the edge of the sea. In fact it is protected by the Scars.

※ The road provides a quiet return route with a character of its own.

• Cresswell has a post-office, shop, café pub and bus terminus.

• <u>Cresswell Tower</u> hides in the trees above the hamlet. Dating from the 14th century it has outlasted its successors built by the Cresswells over the centuries.

101.

Cresswell to Lynemouth 4.5 km (2¾ miles)

Snab Point

Horses are an important part of the local scene. On roadside verges and commons across the district you will see them tethered to graze. Pie-balds seem to be much in favour. These are not the mounts of the rich, or even of teenage girls, but sturdy working horses. Their breeding and maintenance is a long local tradition. Sometimes they can be seen pulling little carts – on land or in the fringes of the sea.

The latter is in conjunction with sea-coaling, another activity local to the north-east. Sea-coal is washed ashore all along the coast. Some is not much larger than dust, and is gathered with a shovel. But some is in decent-sized lumps. Much of this comes from the coal seams that rise in the sea-bed. It burns well – providing what you have is coal rather than black stone! – and there is a thriving local trade, with coalers licensed by British Coal.

Cresswell to Lynemouth.

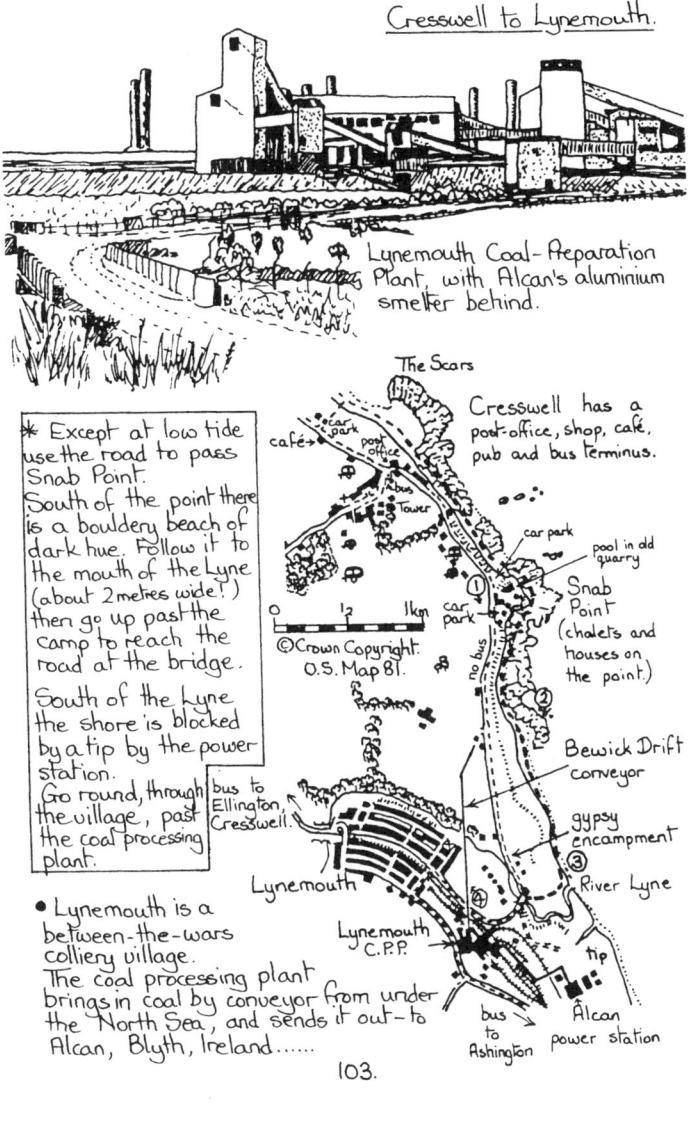

Lynemouth Coal-Preparation Plant, with Alcan's aluminium smelter behind.

Cresswell has a post-office, shop, café, pub and bus terminus.

© Crown Copyright. O.S. Map 81.

* Except at low tide use the road to pass Snab Point.
South of the point there is a bouldery beach of dark hue. Follow it to the mouth of the Lyne (about 2 metres wide!) then go up past the camp to reach the road at the bridge.

South of the Lyne the shore is blocked by a tip by the power station.
Go round, through the village, past the coal processing plant.

• Lynemouth is a between-the-wars colliery village.
The coal processing plant brings in coal by conveyor from under the North Sea, and sends it out to Alcan, Blyth, Ireland......

103.

Lynemouth to Newbiggin Point

4.4km (2¾ miles)

Coal beach, towards Newbiggin.

Some may shut their eyes and scurry past Lynemouth. Some may even give up and catch the bus home. This industry is not beautiful, although it is visually striking. But it is part of the Northumberland scene. The colliery, the aluminium smelter and the power station form part of the industry that still provides the nation's wealth in a way that cosy rurality never could. This provides the relative prosperity that allows us days to go walking.

Alcan power station

Lynemouth to Newbiggin Point.

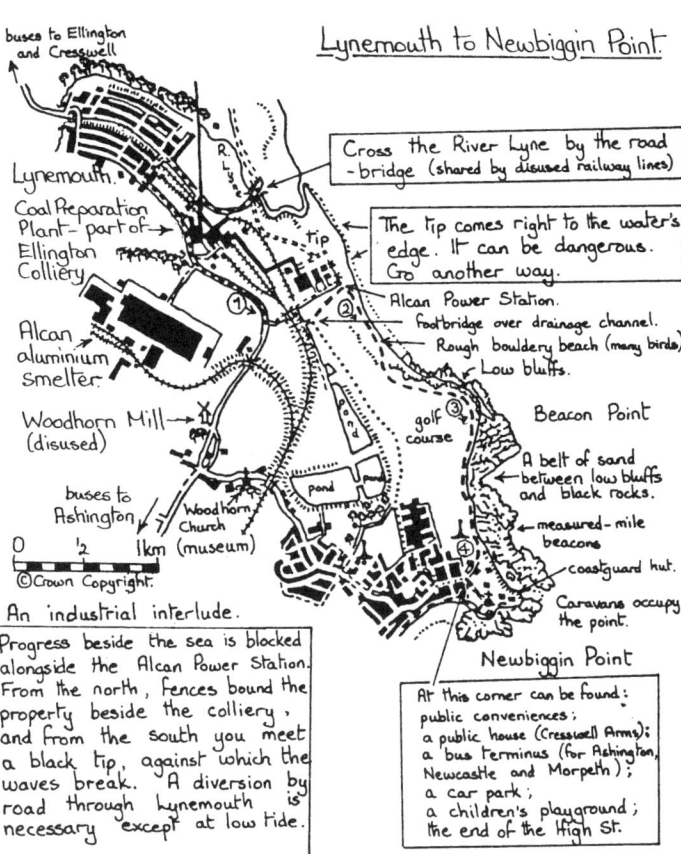

Cross the River Lyne by the road-bridge (shared by disused railway lines)

The tip comes right to the water's edge. It can be dangerous. Go another way.

Alcan Power Station.
- footbridge over drainage channel.
- Rough bouldery beach (many birds).
- Low bluffs.

Beacon Point

A belt of sand between low bluffs and black rocks.

- measured-mile beacons
- coastguard hut.
- Caravans occupy the point.

Newbiggin Point

At this corner can be found:
public conveniences;
a public house (Cresswell Arms);
a bus terminus (for Ashington, Newcastle and Morpeth);
a car park;
a children's playground;
the end of the High St.

An industrial interlude.

*Progress beside the sea is blocked alongside the Alcan Power Station. From the north, fences bound the property beside the colliery, and from the south you meet a black tip, against which the waves break. A diversion by road through Lynemouth is necessary except at low tide.

The path along the seaward side of the golf-course is not a public right of way. It *is* much better than the right of way, which leads from a housing estate across the edge of the dunes, beside tall fencing and taller embankments, to a railway bridge beside the power station. For a return route, the road past Woodhorn Mill and Church is better.

Newbiggin Point enjoys an attractive church, and suffers a sprawling caravan park. The church, and the headland promenade, are worth a visit.

Newbiggin

- St. Bartholomew's, the "church on the point," dates back to the early 13th century. Its spire has been a landmark for North Sea mariners since the 14th century.

From the headland the view south is extensive on a clear day. You can see Blyth, with its great silos and long jetty. Beyond, the slender white column of St. Mary's Island lighthouse can be seen, followed by the tall grey ruins of Tynemouth Priory. The pink and white lighthouse is on Lizard Point, beyond Marsden Bay.

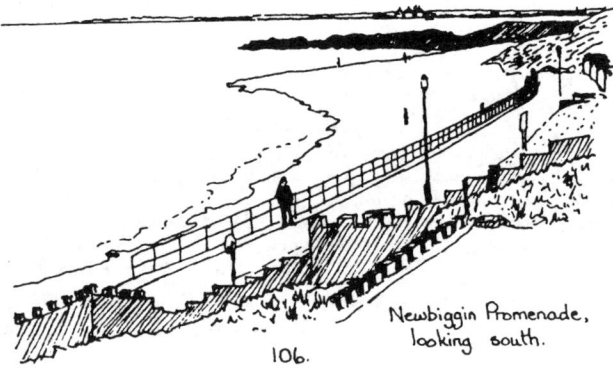

Newbiggin Promenade, looking south.

Newbiggin

- Newbiggin-by-the-Sea is a small seaside town, out of fashion as a resort, and losing much of its sandy beach. Once the sands were much higher – up to the level of the present promenade and sea-wall. The disappearance of the sand left the town exposed to the fury of the sea, and a new sea-wall was built in 1988-90.
The sand is speckled with black-sea coal from seams that outcrop in the beaches north and south of the town. One of the characteristic sights of the area is the sea-coaler, with four or five bags of coal perched on a bicycle.
Newbiggin was a thriving port in mediaeval times, and still is home to a number of the distinctive cobles, with their deep prows and shallow sterns. Tractors go into the surf in all weathers to launch or retrieve them.

Newbiggin Point to the River Wansbeck. 4.5km (2¾ miles)

* Follow the promenade round the bay, past the lifeboat station, & the 'Ship'. At the south end of the bay you can either rise up to the level of the town, and find the footpath that dips into a little valley, or explore the rocks. Find the Needles Eye – a hole in the rocks visible from the far side of the bay). Thence you can make your way up the little valley to join the path.

Climb up southwards past modern residences that guard their privacy with high wire fences and guard-dogs.

The wire-lined channel, leads you to the cliff-edge, and a marvellous view down the coast past the mouth of the river. Cambois power stations dominate the skyline, but closer to hand are the black strata that underlie Newbiggin. The coal is at the foot of the cliffs, and the tops are loose and crumbly. So don't go too near the edge!

As you pass the ranks of caravans of the holiday centre you will find that the cliff-edge path has been eroded, so you will have to divert into the caravan park.

Descend onto the sandy spit that juts out towards Cambois, but DO NOT TRY TO CROSS THE RIVER HERE!
Instead, walk round the bay, under the bridge, to the weir.

108.

Newbiggin Point to the River Wansbeck

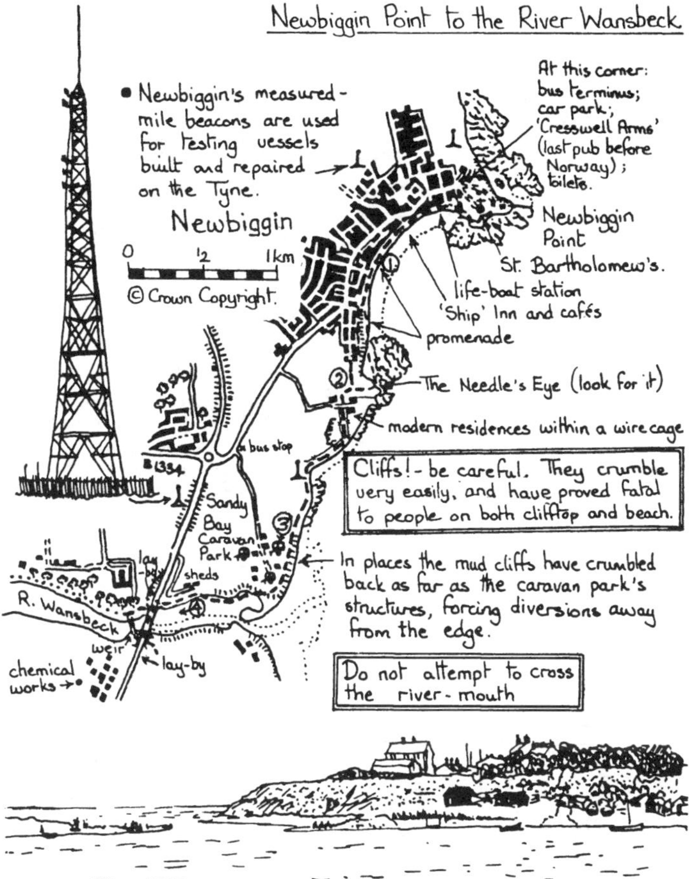

- Newbiggin's measured-mile beacons are used for testing vessels built and repaired on the Tyne.

Newbiggin

0 — ½ — 1km
© Crown Copyright.

At this corner: bus terminus; car park; 'Cresswell Arms' (last pub before Norway); toilets.

Newbiggin Point
St. Bartholomew's
life-boat station
'Ship' Inn and cafés
promenade

The Needle's Eye (look for it)

modern residences within a wire cage

Cliffs! - be careful. They crumble very easily, and have proved fatal to people on both clifftop and beach.

In places the mud cliffs have crumbled back as far as the caravan park's structures, forcing diversions away from the edge.

Do not attempt to cross the river-mouth

bus stop
B1334
Sandy Bay Caravan Park
lay-by
sheds
R. Wansbeck
weir
chemical works
lay-by

Wansbeck Mouth

Wansbeck Mouth.

- The Wansbeck weir and lock form an essential part of the Wansbeck Riverside Park. Before it was built, the river from Sheepwash down had undistinguished boggy banks that were washed and hung up to dry untidily by every tide. Now there are good paths all the way from the river-mouth to Sheep-wash, through well-designed and wooded parkland near Ashington. If you want a major digression, or just a change from beaches, follow the river's north bank upstream past Ashington to Sheepwash. You could even continue across the fields to Bothal, with its castle and Saxon church, both nestling in a wooded elbow of the Wansbeck Valley. Beyond, paths through Bothal Woods would lead you to Morpeth. (and from Sheepwash, Bothal or Morpeth you could even catch a bus back to Newbiggin or Sandy Bay!)

Wansbeck Mouth.

• The mouth of the Wansbeck is a quiet and peaceful place. The points almost meet, leaving a narrow channel to allow the Wansbeck to greet the sea, and enclosing a haven for small boats. On the north side there are solidly-built lock-ups to cater for the sailors and fishermen, whilst on the south side cluster solid but weather-beaten huts, reminiscent of photos of Victorian and Edwardian England. Here men come to relax: work on their boats, fish or enjoy quiet conversation or contemplation. It is difficult to remember that the world of international industry begins just a few hundred metres away (unless the wind happens to be blowing from the direction of the chemicals plant!)

At low tide many of the boats sit on the sand or mud, and a way can be found along the shore on the south side, avoiding the crumbling cliff. But at high tide the water laps right up to the low muddy cliff, making progress difficult: go round!

River Wansbeck to Blyth Ferry   6.5km (4 miles)

The wide beach is backed in places with boulders to inhibit erosion. Behind them is a broad turf, north of the sewer outfall, and grass-bound dunes further south.

- A single-line railway runs behind the dunes, connecting to the Alcan alumina store — the large brown silos that have been prominent in the view for some miles. Several trains run each day, each carrying hundreds of tons of the material to Lynemouth so that it can be made into foil.
- <u>Cambois power</u> station, with its four chimneys, dominates the entire scene of south-east Northumberland. It can be seen from the Cheviots! Its emissions can often be seen drifting along the coast, especially when the Northumberland roke cloaks the coast in cool summer mist. Norwegians also know about Cambois power station.

River Wansbeck to Blyth Ferry.

* From the weir a track passes under the main road, and turns to run alongside it for ½ km, to join the Glaxo access road. Go left, to join the road next to the level crossing. Follow it east

The path along the riverside has crumbled away. It is not a public right of way.

Do not try to ford the river-mouth.

R. Wansbeck
lay-by
Glaxo chemical works.
← bus to Stakeford, Ashington, Alnwick.
Track beside main road
level crossing
coal stock piles:
bus to Bedlington ←
Cambois Power Stations
River Blyth.
mud
mud

Huts and boats of the angling and boating association cluster at the point.
Cars are often parked on the low cliffs.
At the corner are bus-stops (North Blyth – Ashington service) and a mobile toilet. Phone too.
Sewer outfall (Only 1200' long: (it shows!)
British Rail loco. depot
OS Map 81
0 ½ 1km
© Crown Copyright.
Coal exporting staithes (high level).
Grain silos.
'Ridley Arms' P.H.
North Blyth
Blyth Ferry
Old low-level staithes (disused)
Alcan aluminium terminal
The town of Blyth is on this side of the river, here.
Wind turbines (nine)

* As you follow the beach southwards the industry of North Blyth obtrudes very little. Only the alumina silos have a large impact on the eye. (The sewer has a different impact!) But if you desert the beach for the grassy sward or dunes you will get a much better view of this fascinating area.
Follow the sea as far as the jetty, for a view of the harbour approaches and the wind-farm. Return past the Alcan terminal, cross the railway at the crossing and walk down the road past the disused low-level staithes to the Ferry.

Blyth Harbour

- Blyth Harbour is a key part in the economy of south-east Northumberland. It developed with iron, but Bedlington Ironworks closed more than a hundred years ago. Then the coal trade developed enormously, and this continues. The <u>high-level staithes</u> at Cambois (below right) discharge efficiently into colliers, the coal coming by rail from the pits around Ashington and further north, and also from the open-cast mines. The inefficient <u>low-level staithes</u> have outlived their usefulness, and have lost their rails

You may be fortunate enough to watch a large ship enter the harbour, such as the Lord Hinton (above) coming to load coal, and dwarfing the buildings of the town.

Ship-building, a long tradition on the river, has gone. But now there is an <u>alumina terminal</u> (middle, right), where vast quantities are unloaded from ship, stored in the huge silos, and despatched by rail to Lynemouth. A roll-on, roll-off freight terminal for trade with Scandinavia has been developed. Blyth adapts to meet the trade of the times: in 1993 the jetty sprouted a row of wind-turbines.

It is also home to the Royal Northumberland Yacht Club!

The disused lower staithes

Blyth Harbour

Blyth jetty, and the elegant wind-turbines.

The alumina silos

Blyth Ferry to South Beach.   3.2km (2 miles).

*From the 'Ferryman' follow the boundary wall of Wimborne Quay round the corner to the main road. Going towards the centre of town you pass some public toilets, the 'Travellers' Rest Hotel', and the 'Porthole'. Turn left with the main road, bypassing the town centre. A narrow alleyway, just beyond the Marine Engineering yard, offers a way down onto the quay.

Just opposite is the Alcan bauxite terminal, with its great silos and grab hoist. You may be fortunate enough to watch a ship unloading, with hoses playing to lay the dust.

Follow the quay south, past the central concrete section and the wooden staithes. The lifeboat and the Pilot boat berth at the south end. Leave the quay and pass the gate of South Harbour, and walk up to Ridley Park.

• You enter the park past a flower-bed made from a redundant boat, and a triple war-memorial. The park is a delight of lawns and trees, bowling greens and play-areas for kids. There are pavilions for the various clubs, and public toilets. Nor is it locked in by railings. It is a park for people, a place to savour and enjoy.

The park is named after Viscount Ridley, who gave this park to the town. (He was Home Secretary from 1895 to 1900).

*At the South end of the park join the main road. You pass the Ridley Park Hotel, then enter a viewless ½ kilometre: suburban houses on the right, a tall fence bordering a timber yard to the left. Opposite the Wellesley Nautical School you may be able to escape into the South Harbour, to the pier and the beach. Otherwise continue — another ½ km of fence — to two large houses, that mark the start of South Beach.

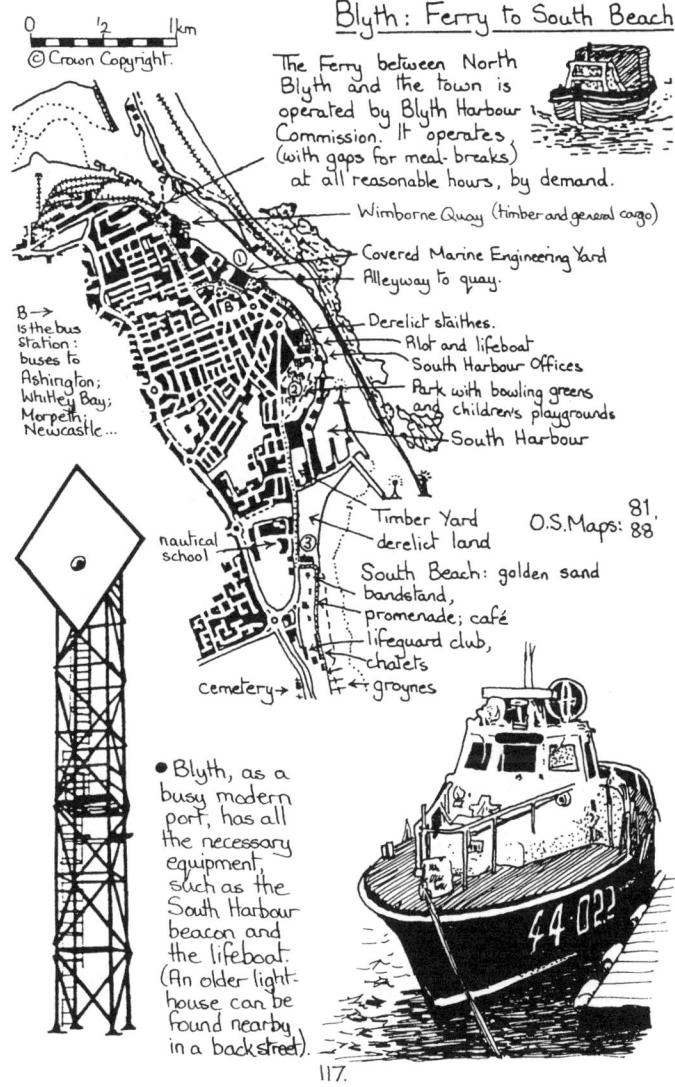

Blyth: Ferry to South Beach

The Ferry between North Blyth and the town is operated by Blyth Harbour Commission. It operates, (with gaps for meal-breaks), at all reasonable hours, by demand.

- Wimborne Quay (timber and general cargo)
- Covered Marine Engineering Yard
- Alleyway to quay.
- Derelict staithes.
- Pilot and lifeboat
- South Harbour Offices
- Park with bowling greens and children's playgrounds
- South Harbour

B → is the bus station: buses to Ashington; Whitley Bay; Morpeth; Newcastle...

O.S. Maps: 81, 88.

- nautical school
- Timber Yard
- derelict land
- South Beach: golden sand
- bandstand,
- promenade; café
- lifeguard club,
- chalets
- groynes
- cemetery →

• Blyth, as a busy modern port, has all the necessary equipment, such as the South Harbour beacon and the lifeboat. (An older lighthouse can be found nearby in a backstreet).

117.

Blyth South Beach to Seaton Sluice.   4.0km (2½ miles).

Blyth South Beach: golden sand & groynes.

Seaton Sluice - the harbour.

- The sluice gates once dammed the river upstream of the present bridge. At low tide, when the harbour bed was exposed, it could be ploughed up using teams of horses. Then the gates were opened and the rush of water took away the silt, maintaining a deep harbour.

Blyth South Beach to Seaton Sluice

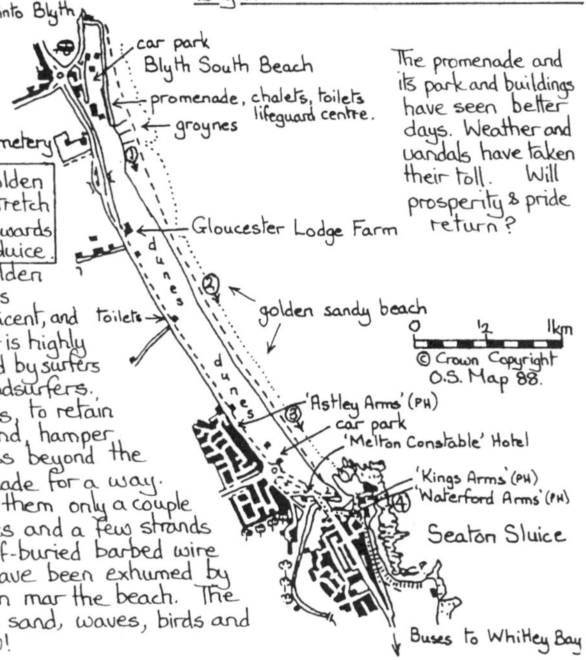

Buses into Blyth

car park
Blyth South Beach
promenade, chalets, toilets
lifeguard centre.
groynes

cemetery

The promenade and its park and buildings have seen better days. Weather and vandals have taken their toll. Will prosperity & pride return?

* The golden sands stretch south towards Seaton Sluice.

Gloucester Lodge Farm

The golden strand is magnificent, and the surf is highly regarded by surfers and windsurfers. Groynes, to retain the sand, hamper progress beyond the promenade for a way. After them only a couple of pipes and a few strands of half-buried barbed wire that have been exhumed by a burn mar the beach. The rest is sand, waves, birds and a view!

toilets
golden sandy beach

0 ½ 1km
© Crown Copyright
O.S. Map 88.

'Astley Arms' (PH)
car park
'Melton Constable' Hotel
'Kings Arms' (PH)
'Waterford Arms' (PH)

Seaton Sluice

Buses to Whitley Bay

Approaching Seaton Sluice.

Seaton Sluice: an industrial past.

- Seaton Sluice is a charming little pleasure-port, with a few small boats riding the Seaton Burn. Grassy banks and houses, plus a collection of public houses present an almost rural picture. Yet for hundreds of years this was an important place of industry, until about 1870.

Hartley Pans was the old name. From the 13th century, when local coal-mining began, the mouth of the burn was the location of huge, coal-fired salt pans, where sea-water was evaporated. This trade flourished until 1782, when the government imposed heavy salt taxes. The legal trade dwindled (and salt-smuggling occurred) until new regulations killed it completely in 1798.

Coal was also shipped from here. By 1660 the harbour was inadequate, and a pier was built to protect the mouth of the harbour. The ingenious sluice followed in 1690, to avoid silting problems. The Delaval family initiated the works (with some government finance). By 1761 more work was necessary, and the cut was blasted through the headland to provide a second harbour entrance.

The extraction of copperas from the pyrites in the local coal measures was also carried on in the town. A major industry, between 1763 and 1871, was the glass-works and bottle-factory. Brick-making, brewing and quarrying were other local industries.

The Gut:

Seaton Sluice

The north harbour-entrance.
(The skyline features chimneys at Cambois and Lynemouth, the Blyth silos and cranes, and St. Bartholomew's at Newbiggin and, now, the wind turbines at Blyth.

Seaton Delaval Hall.

- Seaton Delaval Hall lies a mile up the hill from the roundabout. It is not normally open to the public, but is a grand sight even from the road. Despite extensive fire damage (in 1752 and 1888) it remains a superb example of Vanbrugh's work. It was built (1718-29) for Admiral George Delaval. The family were associated with the area from Norman times, and were responsible for much of the harbour and industrial development of the area. They also had a reputation for gaiety and practical joking. around 1800 — houseguests might find themselves tipped from bed into cold baths, for example!

Seaton Sluice to St. Mary's Island.   2.7km (1¾ miles)

The sea-wall round Collywell Bay. The large stack in the bay is <u>Charlie's Garden</u>. One Charlie Dockwray had an allotment on the top. Despite the exposed site, it reputedly produced the earliest cabbages and potatoes in the village!

Between Seaton Sluice and Curry's Point (opposite St Mary's Island) sandstone cliffs face the pounding seas. These are the scene of many shipwrecks. On 28th October 1880 a ship ran onto the rocks. Thomas Langley, of Hartley, volunteered to be lowered down the cliff-face by rope. He rescued four people. On his way home he heard that another ship had run aground. He seized a line and battled his way through the surf to the ship. All the crew were saved.

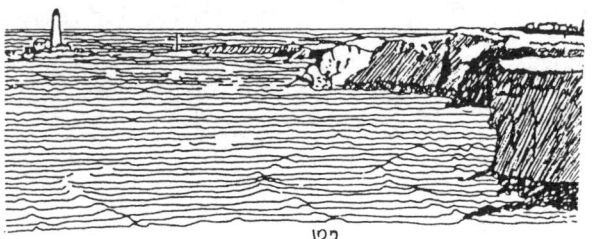

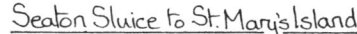

Seaton Sluice to St. Mary's Island.

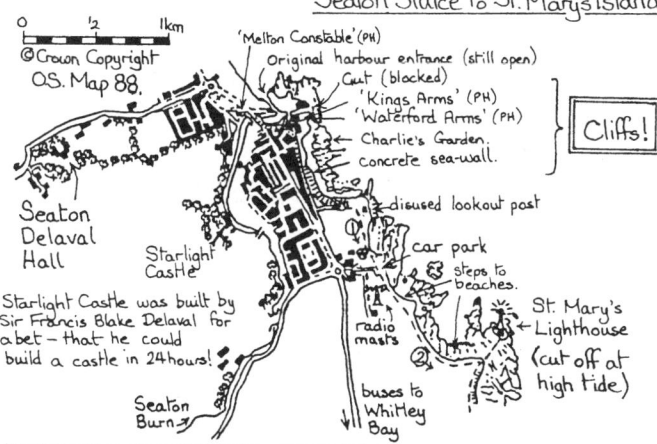

* From the roadbridge over the burn you can follow the harbour side round to the cut, and venture over the bridge onto the peninsula if you wish. But the way south is to follow the old road above the sea-wall. You pass two ways down to the foot of the cliffs, and then, next to a seat, a gateway opens onto a clifftop path.
Follow the path, crossing the beach access road, and cut the corner inland of the derelict lookout post. You pass a caravan site, a car-park and an impressive array of radio-masts. The path continues along the clifftop. Please note the warning signs: the cliff edges are loose and crumbly. Watch your feet whilst moving; STOP to admire the view!

123.

Whitley Bay

Footbridge over Brierdene Burn.

- The pleasure-domes of Whitley Bay: the "Spanish City" contains a permanent fair-ground, with roundabouts, roller-coasters and all sorts of rides, plus games of skill and chance, together with the usual showbiz noise and glitter.

The town of Whitley Bay is built on top of a sandstone cliff, that is now almost invisible under the stone and concrete of the promenades. In winter they are almost deserted, but continue to protect the town. In summer the cafes open, and people throng them.

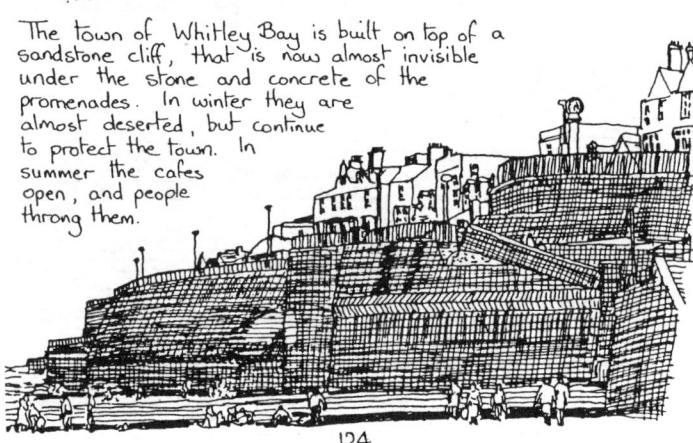

4.5km (2¾ miles)　　St. Mary's Island to Cullercoats Point

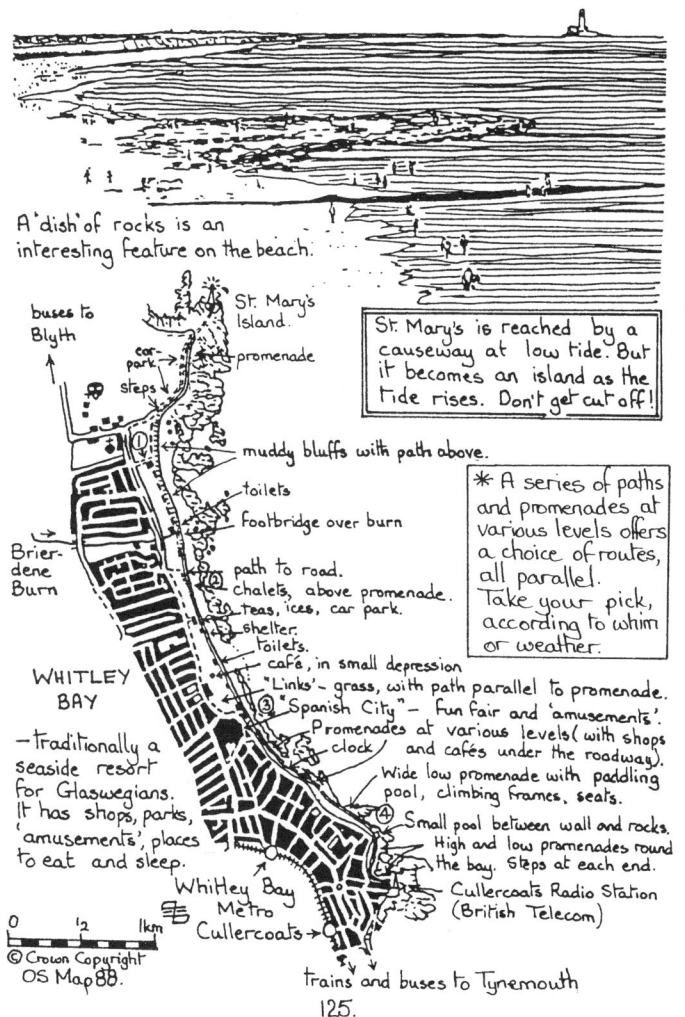

A 'dish' of rocks is an interesting feature on the beach.

buses to Blyth

St. Mary's Island
promenade
car park
steps

St. Mary's is reached by a causeway at low tide. But it becomes an island as the tide rises. Don't get cut off!

muddy bluffs with path above.
toilets
footbridge over burn

Brierdene Burn

path to road.
chalets, above promenade.
teas, ices, car park.
shelter.
toilets.
café, in small depression
"Links" - grass, with path parallel to promenade.
③ "Spanish City" - Fun fair and 'amusements'.
Promenades at various levels (with shops and cafés under the roadway).
clock
Wide low promenade with paddling pool, climbing frames, seats.
④ Small pool between wall and rocks.
High and low promenades round the bay. Steps at each end.
Cullercoats Radio Station (British Telecom)

* A series of paths and promenades at various levels offers a choice of routes, all parallel. Take your pick, according to whim or weather.

WHITLEY BAY
- traditionally a seaside resort for Glaswegians. It has shops, parks, 'amusements', places to eat and sleep.

Whitley Bay Metro
Cullercoats →

0　½　1km
© Crown Copyright OS Map 88.

trains and buses to Tynemouth

125.

Cullercoats

View over the Lifeboat Station.

*Cross Cullercoats Point on the footpath by the Radio Station. This installation, now operated by British Telecom, was one of the earliest marine radio stations when opened in 1908. Go down onto the promenade, and walk along towards the harbour. You pass an electricity board sub-station, in an elegant circular building with a viewing platform on top. It is rather better than the usual offerings!
Climb up again to a higher promenade. Above the Lifeboat Station, decide whether to go down the ramp and cross the harbour floor, or walk round the promenade above the cliff.

Cullercoats.

- The two large buildings on the beach are the <u>Lifeboat House</u> and the <u>Dove Marine Laboratory</u>. The latter is run by Newcastle University and has an aquarium open to the public.

  The harbour is a natural haven, protected by the headlands and the rocky underwater spurs, assisted by the two breakwaters.

---

* On the south side of the harbour, pass the breakwater and the lifeguard's hut onto the headland. Hidden from the main road you will find the <u>Smugglers' Cave</u>, a large natural arch and cave. But Cullercoats is better known as an old fishing port than for smuggling, although the Cullercoats fish-wives no longer carry creels of fish for sale throughout Northumberland.

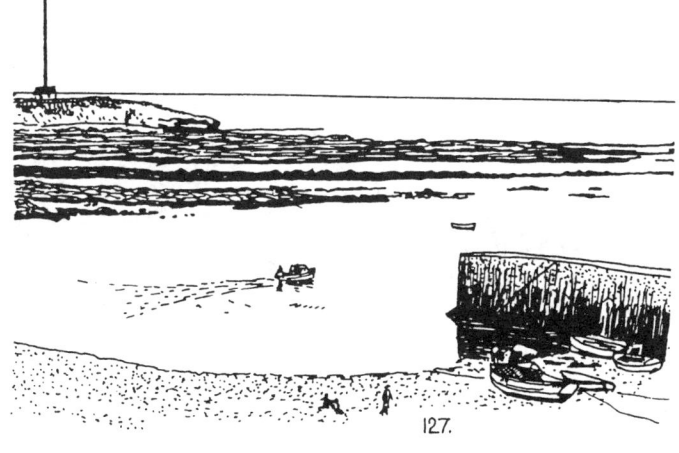

Cullercoats to Tynemouth Priory 2.8km (1¾ mile)

Sharpness Point.

* From the point south of Cullercoats Harbour, follow the beach or the promenade south. You pass St. George's, with its 180' spire. The church is Victorian, reflecting much of Tynemouth housing. The beach is sandy, with cafés, swings and sun-bathers in summer. Above there are green lawns and flowery gardens. The Plaza's grandeur is now host just to amusements and fish and chips. Opposite, the gardens enclose an open-air boating pool. Behind it, the Tyneside Metro runs, the little electric trains providing a fast and efficient service.

An open-air swimming pool nestles below the cliffs as you approach Sharpness Point. Turning the corner, you meet Tynemouth Bay, with its sand, cliffs, steps — and the view of the point, with Priory, Castle and coastguard station

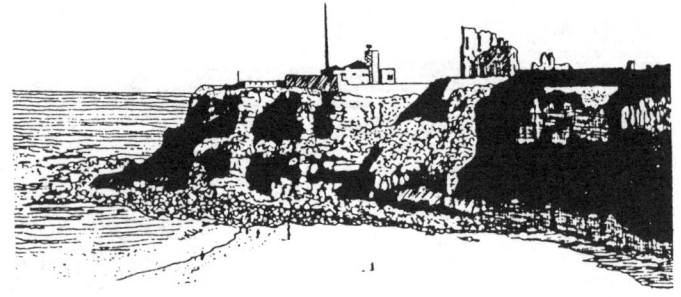

Cullercoats to Tynemouth Priory.

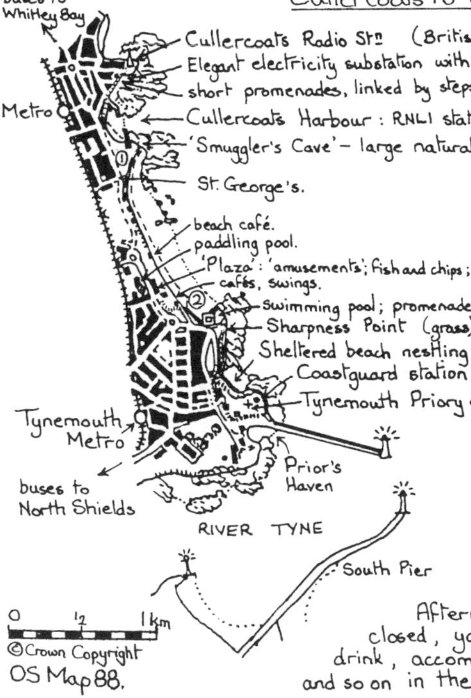

- Cullercoats Radio Stⁿ (British Telecom)
- Elegant electricity substation with viewing gallery.
- short promenades, linked by steps
- Cullercoats Harbour: RNLI station and Dove Marine Lab.
- 'Smuggler's Cave' - large natural arch
- St. George's.
- beach café.
- paddling pool.
- 'Plaza': 'amusements'; fish and chips; *i*
- cafés, swings.
- swimming pool; promenades above.
- Sharpness Point (grass)
- Sheltered beach nestling below steep tall banks.
- Coastguard station
- Tynemouth Priory and Castle

buses to Whitley Bay

Metro

Tynemouth Metro

buses to North Shields

Prior's Haven

RIVER TYNE

South Pier

0   ½   1 km
© Crown Copyright
OS Map 88.

The priory and castle stand on a headland of magnesium limestone. You will want to pay them a visit! (More information is given on the next page). Afterwards, or if they are closed, you can find food, drink, accommodation, transport and so on in the town, just up Front St.

Tynemouth

129.

Tynemouth Castle and Priory.

The headland at Tynemouth is a natural defensive site, walled on three sides by steep cliffs and the sea. It is also important strategically, dominating the mouth of Northumbria's great east-west artery, the River Tyne.

The church recognised the value of the site at an early date, with a religious house here from about 650 AD until Henry VIII dissolved the Priory in 1539.

Fortifications soon developed too. The Priory defended itself from Danish raids, and then from a succession of armies during the Anglo-Scottish wars. It was formally fortified from 1296 (Licence to crenelate). The costs of defence reduced the once-rich Priory to penury.

Henry VIII knew a good thing when he saw it, and took the castle into royal hands when he dissolved the Priory. In Elizabeth's reign the landward slopes were laid out in contemporary style, with artillery positions and anti-siege earthworks. (as at Berwick). It remained a royal castle, and held a garrison until recently. Modern guns were emplaced during the World Wars, and their sites can still be seen, overlooking the North Pier.

- The modern <u>coastguard station</u> was built on the site of the old barracks. Occasionally the Air-Sea Rescue helicopters land here to transfer casualties to ambulances.

Tynemouth Priory.

The coastguard station and Priory, from the west.

The Castle and Priory are in the care of English Heritage, and can be visited during reasonable daylight hours. Entry is along the access road, close under the walls to the Barbican. Inside the curtain wall you find the ruins of the Priory church. Part of the west end, with a fine doorway, and the towering east front, are the prominent features. Beyond the latter, the 15th century Percy Chapel still has its roof, with fine vaulting with carved bosses. The monastic buildings used to lie on the south side of the church, but little remains. To the south-east is a large graveyard. Amongst the gravestones is one for Corporal Rotto, who held the lantern for the burial of Sir John Moore at Corunna. Do visit the eastern ramparts, for the view of the mouth of the mighty Tyne.

The Castle Barbican.

Tynemouth to North Shields Fish Quay

* From the end of Front Street, opposite the Castle Barbican, go down the road towards the river. Turn left at the foot of the bank and head for the North Pier. If conditions allow, walk out to the end.

• The view is excellent: the headland itself; the river-mouth; the coast stretching northwards past St. Mary's lighthouse; the coast to the south along the rising cliffs to candy-striped Souter Light. The piers were built to allow ships to leave the rivermouth in unfavourable conditions. Started in 1854, they had poor foundations and were damaged badly by storms. They were completed in 1890, breached two years later, then rebuilt.

* Return to the shore. The haven on the left, used by a sailing club, is Prior's Haven. Cross the line of the railway that used to connect with the North Eastern up in town. Now you have a choice of routes: either follow the road onto the promontory and go down past the Life Brigade Watch House onto the riverside path; or follow a footpath to the right, past the Collingwood Monument.

• The Life Brigade was established here to save lives, after a series of horrific wrecks on the Black Middens. These lurk just below the surface at high tide, on the north of the river.
• The Collingwood Memorial commemorates Nelson's second-in-command at Trafalgar, who was born in Newcastle.

* Choose from the variety of paths to lead you to N. Shields.

Watch out for:
• the High and Low Lights: white lighthouses marking the passage.
• the South Shields Groyne, tipped with a squat red lighthouse. The groyne was built to prevent the rivermouth silting up.
• the Lifeboat Station (too small to contain the present boat).
• the Pilot boat (and moorings at South Shields).
• Clifford's Fort, built in 1672 to protect the river from the Dutch Navy. Now it contains kipper-houses, and the Low Light.
• the Fish Quay, home for the North Shields fishing fleet.

4.6 km (2¾ miles).   <u>Tynemouth to North Shields</u>

The "Esso Severn", a coastal tanker, enters the River Tyne past the Fish Quay (1986). Tyne Street, up by the High Light, is a superb vantage point for watching the river.

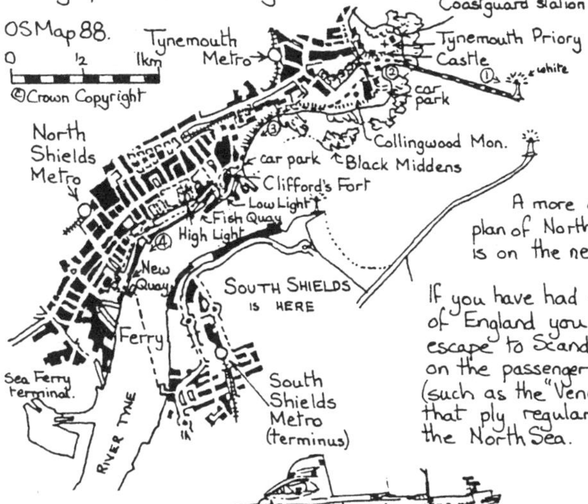

OS Map 88.

A more detailed plan of North Shields is on the next page.

If you have had enough of England you could escape to Scandinavia on the passenger ferries (such as the "Venus," below) that ply regularly across the North Sea.

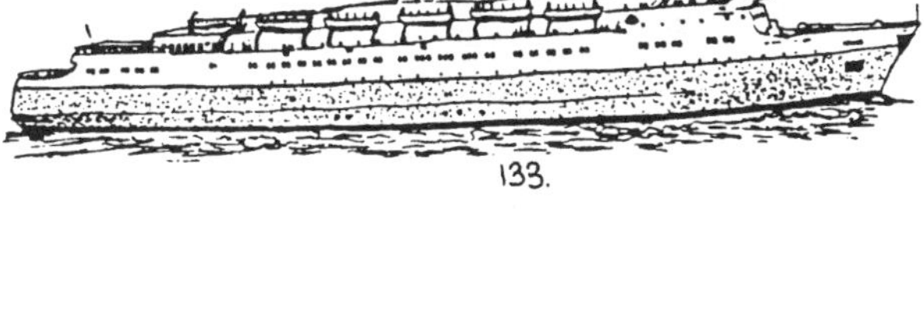

North Shields

- The High and Low Lights at North Shields are leading lights. When lined up they indicate the deep-water passage for ships entering or leaving the Tyne. The sand-banks shift over the years, so there has been a succession of lights since 1540. The present High Light (up on Tyne Street) and Low Light (down next to the Fish Quay) are dated 1808 on their stonework. A plaque recalls their rebuilding in 1860. Operation is automatic.

- The Old High Light was built in 1727 by Trinity House. Note that the seaward side is painted black to avoid confusion with the present High Light.

The steep banks below the Lights were once crammed with houses clustering around the many flights of steps that still link the two levels. Conditions were appalling, with only rudimentary water and sewage services. The banks were cleared in the 1930s and are now covered in grass, bushes and trees.

The area between Tyne Street and the main town has also been covered in slums in the past. The most recent (built 1956) have now been pulled down, and new houses have been built (1987).

North Shields: Fish Quay to Stag Line.

Old North Shields:
(NOT to scale)

[Map labels: Old High Light, Trinity Bldgs, "Wooden Doll", "New Dolphin", Clifford's Fort, Lifeboat House, Low Light, High Light, steps, "Stag Line" pub, Port buildings, Fish Quay, Western Quay, Tiger Stairs, Greave's Stairs, "Prince of Wales", Dolphin Quay: Flats, The "Haddock Shop", Yeoman Street, RIVER TYNE, Borough Road, footbridge, "Porthole", "Northumberland Arms", New Quay: car park, New housing, "Chain Locker", Ferry Landing, Bus Terminus, Smith's Dock]

* From the Fish Quay you could choose to follow the quayside and the Low Street along to the Ferry Landing. But the best route is along the top of the bank:
Cross the road and climb the steps up the bank to the 'Wooden Doll' public house. Follow the road westwards, passing Trinity Buildings, the Old High Light and the present High Light. Looking down the bank you can look over the roofs of the riverside buildings (including the Fish Quay, & the Custom House).
It is a superb place for watching the river.
Continue along Tyne Street to the old Library (the Stag Line public house) and enjoy the view from the balcony above the steps: the Library Flags.

- The 'Wooden Doll' public house:
This is named after the succession of wooden dolls (ships' figureheads and statues of fishwives) that have stood in North Shields since about 1814.

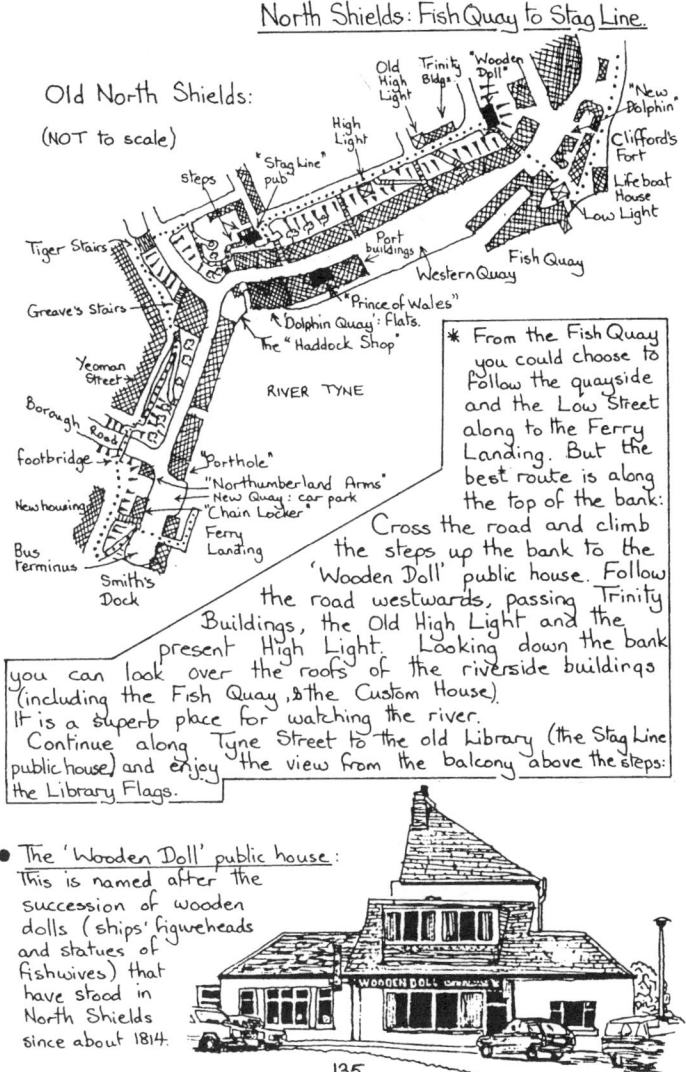

135.

North Shields.

- <u>The Stag Line building</u>
was built in 1806-7 as a library, by the Literary & Philosophical Society of Tynemouth. The Stag Line shipping company took it over in 1895, and used it until 1980. The company emblem still proudly overlooks the river from the south wall. Now it is the 'Stag Line' public house.
The balcony outside, the Library Flags, is a superb viewpoint. Read the inscription above the steps that go down to the river.
- Down below, the "<u>Haddock Shop</u>", once a specialist repair yard for light-vessels, is being redeveloped. Half is now under "Dolphin Quay", a late 1980s Docklands-style riverside condominium.

North Shields: Stag Line to New Quay

* Go down the steps on the NORTH side of the Stag Line pub, down Ranter's Bank. The stairs twist and turn past buildings long gone, down to a garden just above Liddell St. A footpath leads across and then up Magnesia Bank. Follow it up to Union St. Turn left, briefly down to Bedford St, then straight ahead up Tiger Stairs. Go left past new housing and the top of Greave's Stairs and past Olivers Engineering works. Either walk along Yeoman St, or the terrace just below, to the bridge over Borough Rd. (a toll road cut by the Railway to link ferry and station). Past the bridge go on past more new housing to a vantage point overlooking Smith's Dock — the heart of Tyneside ship repair work.

A ramp goes down to the bus terminus, New Quay and the ferry.

The Stag Line building, from Liddell Street (1986)

Shields Ferry

If you have enjoyed the coastline of Northumberland, you will probably also enjoy its continuation southwards along the edge of the old County Durham: South Shields, Frenchman's Bay, Marsden Rock and Roker Sands await your delectation.

The Shields Ferry is the first stage in a new adventure... or the last stage in this one: cross the Tyne by ferry to see this river from the proper angle — there is plenty of public transport in South Shields to take you home!

Bibliography

These books have proved informative and entertaining, and as such are suggested for further reading:

'Lindisfarne'   Magnus Magnusson, Oriel, (R+KP) 1984.
'Northumberland' Nikolaus Pevsner + Richmond, Penguin 1957.
'Portrait of Northumberland', Nancy Ridley, Robert Hale 1965.
'Northumbrian Heritage'   Nancy Ridley, Robert Hale 1968.
'Northumbria'   Harold Wade, Geographia
'The Long Bay of Druridge'   Henry Tegner, Frank Graham 1968.
'Northumberland Villages'   Godfrey Watson, Robert Hale 1976.
'Northumbria'   Edward Grierson, Collins 1976.
'Northumbria in Pictures', Beryl Sanderson, Sandhill
'Discovering Northumberland' T.H. Rowland, Frank Graham 1973.
'Northumberland: the Queens England', Arthur Mee, N. County, 1952.
'Highways and Byways in Northumberland', P. Anderson Graham, Macmillan 1921.
'Companion into Northumberland' Sydney Moorhouse, Methuen 1953.
'Ramblers through Northumberland' Ramblers Assoc., F.Graham 1977.
'Walks on the Northumberland Coast' N. County Council 1983.
'Curiosities of Northumberland', J.Armstrong, F.Graham, T.H.Rowland Frank Graham 1970
'Holy Island', M. Scott Weightman   1983.
'Looking Around Northumberland', Harry Rowland   1979
'Dunstanburgh Castle' C.H. Hunter Blair, English Heritage 1988
'Warkworth Castle' Honeyman + Blair, English Heritage 1988
'Seaton Delaval Hall'
'Walker's Britain'   Ordnance Survey + Pan Books 1982.
'Walker's Britain 2'   Ordnance Survey + Pan Books 1986
'Birdwatcher's Britain' Paslow, O.S. + Pan Books 1983.
'Ordnance Survey Leisure Guide: Northumbria, AA/OS 1987.
'The Reivers' Way,' H.O. Wade, Frank Graham 1977.
'Songs and Ballads of N. England' T+G Allan (Newcastle)
'North Shields Riverside Trail' Tyne + Wear County Council.
'A Story of Amble' Wilkinson + Morrison, Amble Council.
'A History of Embleton Parish Church' Oswin Craster, Embleton P.C.
'The Natural History of Dunstanburgh Castle Point,' Sir John Craster HMSO 1963.
'Walks for Motorists - 'Northumberland', R.A., F.Graham 1981.
'The Wildlife of Northumbria' William Balmain, F.Graham 1971.
'North Northumberland for the Walker,' Wade + Balmain, N. Gazette.
'Northumbria Walks'   O.S. / Jarrold   1991.
'Hartley and Old Seaton Sluice' Thomas Earnshaw   1961.

Index

Alcan. 103-5, 112-3.
Aln. 84-5
Alnmouth. 81-85.
Alnmouth station. 85-87
Alnwick.
Amble. 94-97
.... Braid. 95
Ashington. 110

Bamburgh. 48-55
.... Castle. 49-54
Bathing House, Howick. 10, 75, 79
Beachcomber House. 28
Beadnell. 60-65
Beal. 29, 30
Belford. 47
Berwick. 9, 14-22
.... Castle. 16-17
.... Ramparts. 19-21
Blakemoor Farm. 101
Blyth. 4, 112-117
...... Ferry. 113, 117
Boulmer. 79-81
Budle Bay. 46-49
Budle Point. 48, 49

Cambois. 112-113
Chare Ends. 31
Charlie's Garden. 122
Cheswick. 28
Church Hill, Alnmouth. 82-83
Cocklawburn. 26
Collingwood Monument. 132
Coquet. 86-96
Coquet Island. 97
Craster. 73-75
.... Tower. 73
Cresswell. 100-103
Cullercoats. 8, 126
Cullernose Point. 75

Druridge 99-101
Druridge Bay 98-101
Dunstanburgh
.... Castle, 66, 69-73

Ebba's Chapel. 61, 62
Elwick. 43-45
Embleton. 67, 68
Emmanuel Head. 38, 42

Farne Islands. 57-59
Fenham. 40-43
.... Flats. 40-43
Fenham-le-Moor. 40-43
Fenwick Stead. 42, 43
Fish Quay. 133, 135
Football Hole. 64

Goswick. 29
Grace Darling. 51, 59
Grizell Cochrane. 43
Guile Point. 37, 44

Hauxley. 97
Hermitage. 90
The Heugh, Holy Island 35
Heughs, Craster. 73
High Lights, Shields. 11, 132, 134
Hipsburn. 85
Holy Island. 30-39
Howick 75
.... Hall. 75-79

Inner Farne. 55, 58, 59
Islestone. 55

Lesbury. 84-85
Lindisfarne Castle. 36
Lindisfarne Priory. 32, 33
Long Nanny.
Longstone. 59
Low Lights. 11, 132, 134
Low Newton. 64-66
Lynemouth. 103-105

Marshall Meadows. 14
Morpeth. 110

Needle's Eye. 14, 108
Newbiggin. 106-108

140.

Index

North Low. 29
North Shields. 11, 133-138.

Old Law. 45.

Ridley Park. 116
Ross. 45, 47
Ross Back Sands. 44-47
Royal Border Bridge. 16
Royal Tweed Bridge. 18, 22
Rumbling Kern. 6, 78.

Saddle Rock. 69.
St. Aidan's, Bamburgh. 50.
St. Bartholomew's. 106.
St Cuthbert. 33-4, 57, 97
St. Cuthbert's Isle. 34
St. Lawrence, Warkworth. 90-1
St. Mary's Island. 122-125.
Sandstell Point. 23-25
Scremerston. 25
Seahouse, Scremerston. 25
Seahouses 55-6, 60-1.
Seaton Delaval Hall 121.

Seaton Sluice. 118-122.
Shields Ferry. 138.
Snook Tower. 31.
the Skaith. 67, 69
South Low. 29, 31.
South Shields. 133, 138.
Spittal. 22-25
Stag Rock. 49
Staple Island. 58
Starlight Castle. 107

Tweed.
Tweedmouth. 22
Tyne. 129-138
Tynemouth. 129-132
.... Priory. 128-131
.... Castle. 128-131

Wansbeck. 108-113
Waren Mill. 47
Warkworth. 88-94
.... Castle, 7, 92-94
Whitley Bay. 124.
Widdrington. 99
Wooden. 87
Woodhorn. 105.

---

beacons 44, 80, 96, 109, 117
beaches almost every page.
castles 7, 16, 36, 49-54, 66, 69-72, 128-131.
causeways 29-31, 39, 125
churches 32, 34, 50, 59, 62, 68, 84, 90-1, 106, 128-131
harbours 7, 14, 56, 63, 73, 80, 94-5, 107, 114-5, 120, 126.
lifeboat stations 22, 80, 107, 117, 127, 132.
lighthouses 4, 11, 15, 49, 55, 56, 59, 97, 122-3, 134.
limekilns 27, 37, 63.
mills 47.
power stations, 4, 104, 108, 112, 115.
radio stations 65, 123, 127
railway stations 13, 16, 85-7, 125, 129.
stately homes 76, 121
wind turbines. 4, 115.

SYMBOLS USED ON THE SKETCH MAPS.

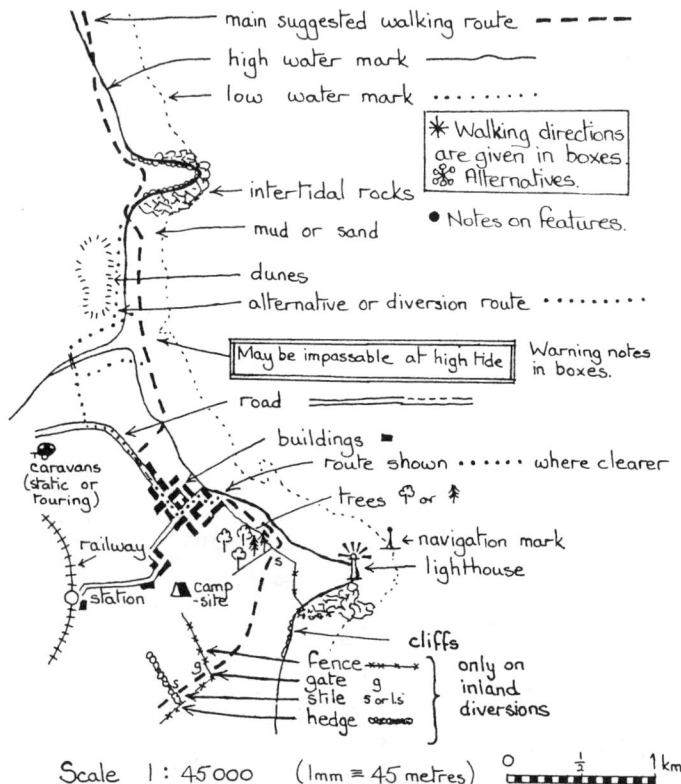

Scale 1 : 45000   (1mm ≡ 45 metres)   0 — ⅓ — 1 km

The routes shown are not necessarily rights of way. There are some permissive paths, and some rights of way. For specific information use the Ordnance Survey maps.

Remember too that things change. The coast-line is very active. Erosion can change cliffs, alter coastal streams, destroy paths. New paths may be agreed, or others closed.

Personal notes.

This page is for your use, perhaps to record when you visited various parts of the coast, perhaps to jot down the name of those nice people you met. Perhaps you will use it to note grumbles! But if I write too many suggesthions there will be no space left!

Northern Heritage Services Limited
Publisher of local books and DVDs
www.northern-heritage.co.uk

● The Author.

Odd as it may seem, Ian Smith is not a native of these parts. Although he has been in love with Northumberland — and one of its girls — for over twenty years, he actually lives in Thornaby, on the Tees. His origins are even further afield, not even in the North: he hales from Bromley in Kent! Having destroyed some people's illusions, he hastily adds that he much prefers the North, and Northumberland in particular!
Ian is a physics teacher, daily in touch with a high technology world of equipment and computing. The walking, photography, drawing and hand-writing is a nice contrast.